THE
UPROOTED

THE
UPROOTED

by
Charles Paul May

w

THE WESTMINSTER PRESS
PHILADELPHIA

BOOK DESIGN BY DOROTHY E. JONES

PUBLISHED BY THE WESTMINSTER PRESS®
PHILADELPHIA, PENNSYLVANIA

PRINTED IN THE UNITED STATES OF AMERICA

Library of Congress Cataloging in Publication Data

May, Charles Paul.
  The uprooted.

  Bibliography: p.
  Includes index.
  SUMMARY: Traces America's role in the forced migration
of minorities from the forced importation of conscripts
and indentured servants in colonial days to the present
day evacuation of urban dwellers.
  1. Minorities—United States—History—Juvenile
literature. 2. United States—Emigration and immigration—History—Juvenile literature. 3. Migration,
Internal—United States—History—Juvenile literature.
[1. Minorities. 2. United States—Emigration and immigration—History] I. Title.
E184.A1M34   301.32'9   75–42255
ISBN 0–664–32591–2

CONTENTS

INTRODUCTION

We think nothing of transplanting rice or other growing vegetation. When we remove tomato seedlings from a box where they have started to sprout and place them in a garden where they'll have more room, we help them to thrive. They repay us by developing large, juicy fruits, which they couldn't do if we left them in the box.

The white rhinoceros of Africa has become rare. Scientists fear that it will die out if left in its usual region of South Africa, so they are experimenting with transplanting it to other areas. They forcibly remove it from its regular habitat and make it start a new life hundreds to thousands of miles away. If this saves it from extinction, we will proudly feel that relocation was the right decision.

But what about people? Can some men forcibly relocate others and expect almost everybody to benefit?

Our health, mental and physical, throughout life is determined to a great extent by our relationships with human beings in our own group. According to psychologists who have made it their business to observe young animals and children during their earliest years, the way our mothers, fathers, close relatives, and neighbors treat us when we are young can make the difference between happiness and misery for us, perhaps for the rest of our lives.

As social beings from the start, tender and helpless in our early years, we are dependent on those around us to provide food, clothing, and shelter and teach us the simple virtues of human kindness that we will imitate later in our turn. As social beings we also need reassurance that we are appreciated and trusted. We need the approval of other human beings to help us attain a sense of identity. And in reaching out to explore the world, we need a gradually expanding area of space with objects in it that we can investigate before returning safely home to our parents. This is our territory. Later, it expands as our maturing years introduce us to larger and more varied circles of human acquaintances. We develop a loyalty to what is familiar and safe and provides our needs. If anything or anybody threatens our autonomy or possessions there, our security is threatened and we react defensively.

Almost from the founding of the first English settlement in the New World, tearing up groups from their territories has played a part in North American history. We might try to excuse our ancestors by saying that their times were different and that they knew no better than to tamper with other men's lives. But how do we excuse ourselves? Right down to the 1970's, we have gone on forcing people to leave one place and settle in another. Did some of these moves work out well enough to help keep the practice alive? Are there any yardsticks for determining whether a move will be beneficial or not? These are questions this book will undertake to answer.

What exactly do we mean by forced relocation? Did James Edward Oglethorpe herd debtors from England's prisons onto ships and make them come to the New World against their own wishes? No, they had to express an interest in coming to America. Even then they could not undertake the trip until their stories and backgrounds had been thoroughly checked. If a man proved to be better off than he pretended and the investigators found out, they turned him down. A man with a reputation for being lazy

8

or a talent for wasting money had little chance of acceptance. So the men who helped Oglethorpe to found Georgia do not fit the forced-to-move classification.

What about the Puritans? One of England's kings said he would harry them out of the land. He did not, however, say he would have them gathered up bodily and shipped abroad whether they chose to go or not. In his mind, he gave them a choice. They could accept his views on religion or they could leave. So each Puritan's conscience played a part in determining the move he made. He was driven from within himself as well as from outside and so cannot be linked with the men and women who had no choice in moving.

A person who is forced to relocate is one who has to go no matter what his own wishes are. On the surface it sounds like cruel and inhuman treatment. This book will help us decide if all cases are that, if none of them are, or if some are inhuman while others are beneficial.

*To Charles, Katy, Mary Ann,
Brian, and Kevin.*

*Also to Fran Ellen,
Chuck, and family.*

1
SPIRITED
TO AMERICA
Colonial Conscripts

Many men, women, and children came to the New World as the victims of kidnappers. During the 1600's in the British Isles and on the Continent, several periods proved to be times of hardship. Landowners began to fence in acreages in order to raise sheep because wool brought a good price. Whereas many men had been needed to plow the soil and raise crops, only a few were needed now to tend large flocks of sheep. This threw hundreds of farm laborers out of work. Improved machinery in factories created additional unemployment. The 1660's and 1690's were especially troubled decades. The 1600's were also the years in which the North American continent received its first permanent English settlements.

Among the early New World colonists could be found farmers, blacksmiths, candlemakers, carpenters, tailors, bootmakers, and other men with some degree of skill in a useful trade. Often lacking were the ordinary laborers needed to help these craftsmen and landowners. Since unemployment was high in the British Isles and elsewhere in Europe and since workers were badly needed in the colonies, many people considered it logical to transport laborers to the New World. Some of the poor of England, Ireland, Scotland, and other parts of Europe welcomed the chance for a new start across the sea, but their numbers failed to eliminate entirely the labor shortage.

As a result, a few officials, or agents, who had the task of recruiting workers began to use unfair means when their glowing reports and advertisements of life abroad no longer attracted people to sign up for service in the New World. An unemployed man or an orphan boy might be hit over the head in some dark street and carried aboard a ship while he was unconscious. Women as well as men and boys could be given so much wine to drink that they passed out. When they awoke, they found themselves in the stinking hold of a ship riding west before the wind.

Girls and boys often made the mistake of accepting candies from kindly-looking women. These women promised more sweets or a good meal if the youngsters wanted to accompany them to their homes, which many half-starved children eagerly did. Some youngsters may have noticed that they were being led into streets where a respectable woman would be unlikely to venture. Perhaps they guessed that something was wrong and fled before they could be trapped. But others, with the sugary taste of candy fresh on their tongues, followed along past empty, boarded-up houses, noisy taverns, and smelly stables. One unsavory section of London boasted the sacred-sounding name of St. Katherine's. It lay east of the famous royal prison, the Tower, and stretched along the Thames River. It proved to be an excellent place to load cargoes onto ships without being observed. Another area in which kidnappings occurred was Middlesex County, also on the Thames, which joined London on the west. Middlesex court records say that an "inticer of children" led her victims to "obscure haunts." Probably the woman leading a youngster stopped at a building that had all the windows boarded over. The door swung open when the woman knocked, but as the girls or boys entered they were grabbed from behind, rough hands closing over their mouths to keep them from calling for help.

12

From hearing sniffles or sobs in the dark room, a captive would learn that others shared the same fate. The buildings usually stood far enough away from occupied dwellings that the moans and whimpers of frightened youngsters reached no sympathetic ears. If any people did hear, they either had little concern for what went on or feared for their own safety if they became involved. The kidnappers, known as kidnabbers or spirits (because they spirited people out of the country), hoped to place their victims on a ship within a few days. They fed them little—sometimes hardly more than bread and water—to hold down the expenses as much as possible.

Usually after a day to a few days in a boarded-up building, the victims were taken at night in small groups through the streets to a ship. However, from tales some kidnap victims later told, we know that delays of a month or more occurred at times. Sea captains who dealt in such human cargo wanted to fill their holds in a hurry and therefore paid a price for each person without asking any questions. Those seamen who later found themselves in trouble claimed they assumed that all the people brought to their ship had signed papers agreeing to go to the colonies. The price that captains paid in the middle 1600's amounted to a pound or two per individual. We cannot compare this with dollars, for at that time the colonies had no local currency. They used British coins and, because of trade with the West Indies, Spanish ones.

Few of the kidnapped adults, let alone the young people, were able to write and thus could not leave records of their experiences. One man who did leave a report claimed to be the son of a landowner but he was more interested in proving his right to an estate than in telling what had happened after he had been taken prisoner. We can be sure the spirits, or kidnappers, wanted no records left. As a result, the names of most captives are unknown. Even the identities of spirits are questionable. In 1645 two men accused Margarett Emmerson of Middlesex of being a spirit. When she denied the charge they knocked her about, which landed them, rather than her, in court. Unable to prove their accusations against her, they paid fines while she went free. In a similar case, also in Middlesex County, a woman attacked Mary Hodges for luring children away. Mary escaped punishment, but the woman who tried to harm her faced a charge of starting a riot. The Middlesex court records show many cases of women and men being tried for spiriting, but few convictions resulted.

Conditions aboard the ships carrying human cargo often proved nearly unbearable. A few ships were so leaky they had to return to the British Isles, and the captives either escaped or were discovered by law-enforcement officers and so gained their freedom. In some instances, four hundred or more people found themselves crowded aboard vessels qualified to carry less than half that many. Even when people signed papers agreeing to come willingly, dishonest captains gave them less space than contracts called for. Diseases broke out and deaths among captives occurred frequently. When anyone died, the person's belongings fell to members of the crew and the body was thrown overboard.

Upon reaching port in the colonies, the captain promptly advertised his cargo in local papers, by having dock workers spread the word, or by nailing printed announcements to trees, posts, and buildings. He generally said the cost of transporting each person amounted to six to ten pounds, so to make a profit he asked ten to twenty pounds for an individual. Strong people and young ones brought more than older or feeble-looking ones. A handsome girl could be sold for more than a homely one. With far more men than women in the colonies—Virginia at one time reportedly had a ratio of sixty-five to one—even the most unattractive girl would be purchased. In time, if she didn't run away and wasn't beaten to death for disobedience, she married, but not until after she had served her time unless her master gave his consent.

A girl who appeared to have a better-than-usual background brought a higher price than girls who were ignorant and ill-bred. As a result, one kidnabber concocted the idea of spiriting away daughters from upper-class British households. He expected to make his fortune in a hurry. Perhaps he failed to take into account that most orphans on the streets had no one to notice if they disappeared, or that a very poor family might not be altogether brokenhearted when there was one less mouth to feed. But wealthier families kept closer account of their children, and the dealer soon ended his life at the end of a prison rope. Few spirits suffered such a punishment, and some grew wealthy.

Supposedly men, women, and children who were brought to the New World as laborers did not become slaves. They were indentured, or signed over, to masters —to the ones who paid for their passage on the ship. Usually a period of indenture ran for four or five years, but some lasted as long as fourteen. A child of nine or ten, who supposedly could do less work than someone older, might have a longer term than the average seven years. An indentured servant was expected to do whatever the master requested, to stay away from taverns and playhouses, and "to keep the master's secrets." The master provided food, lodging, and two sets of clothing, one for everyday wear and one for Sunday.

Not all people who wanted indentured servants could afford to pay the ten or more pounds, but they might have goods to barter. Captains sometimes accepted sugar, rum, sassafras root, tobacco, or lumber. In 1675 Captain Benjamin Cooper received more than 3,000 acres of land in Maryland for 71 servants. Being a seagoing man, he did not choose to wait around long enough to sell the land bit by bit for the huge profit he could have earned. Instead, he sold it to a local businessman for what he considered a satisfactory return, and the businessman broke it down into several farms, from which he made a fortune.

15

Many indentured servants, both those who agreed to come and those who had no choice, became discontented after they arrived. Under their terms of indenture, they had to work four to fourteen years to pay for a passage that had cost less than twenty pounds. Yet they saw free laborers around them earning twelve pounds and more for one year of work. Many servants ran away, either to live with Indian tribes or to reach other settlements, where they claimed they were free individuals. Masters constantly advertised in newspapers and with broadsides for runaway indentured servants.

Some of the people who were brought to the colonies proved to be as tricky as the spirits themselves. After arriving in the New World, these laborers claimed they had been kidnapped. If they got a local court to uphold their charges, they went free and the captains who brought them might have to pay fines. In any case, the captains were out whatever money they had paid to legitimate agents or to spirits back in Europe.

Robert Louis Stevenson wrote a famous novel that involved an attempt to spirit a boy out of the British Isles. Appropriately enough, he titled it *Kidnapped*. In it, a cruel uncle wants to get rid of young David Balfour because the boy is the rightful heir to the castle occupied by the uncle. After the uncle closes a deal with an untrustworthy sea captain, David is lured on board the ship, knocked unconscious, and started on a series of adventures that make exciting reading.

As early as 1645, Parliament legislated against spiriting. Since the practice was lucrative, the law went unheeded. During the late 1600's and throughout the 1700's, more and more thinking people of the British Isles and other parts of Europe began to recognize the injustices of spiriting and deportation. They began to fight particularly for the rights of young people, finally causing new laws to be passed against forced relocation. Again officials often ignored the regulations, except during periods of strong

16

public protest. At such times, law-enforcement officers boarded ships from which the cries of children could be heard, and a captain who tried to prevent them became subject to arrest. Some ships underwent search even after they had left port, and many victims of spiriting got safely back to shore. But despite the changing attitude toward forms of forced relocation, kidnapping and deportation continued past the period of the American Revolution, ending with the War of 1812.

A youngster might escape the treachery of a kidnabber and still be forced to move, as was the case with Molly Welsh. In 1698 this girl served a family on an estate in Wessex, where her duties included doing the milking. Perhaps Molly tried to become too friendly with the master of the house and got caught by his wife, who decided to have the girl sent far away at the first opportunity. Or perhaps Molly wouldn't become as friendly as the master wanted, and he decided to get rid of her so he could hire a more cooperative girl in her place. Both of these things happened at times. Maybe Molly was really guilty of the crime of which someone on the estate accused her, but stealing one pail of milk sounds like a forgivable crime if the family had really wanted to keep her.

Molly found herself dragged into court on the charge that she had stolen the milk. She claimed the cow had kicked her off the stool and upset the pail, causing all its contents to spill before she could right it. Without a witness, her story had to stand against that of a well-known family, a family that could slip the presiding officer some money to influence his decision if necessary. No records exist to tell what truly happened, but Molly failed to save herself from being deported to North America, where she served for seven years as an indentured servant.

Not everybody who was moved against his will was a child or a teen-ager. As early as 1611, only three years after the founding of Jamestown, Virginia, some men in the British government suggested cleaning out the jails of

17

England by sending prisoners of all ages to the New World. In 1617, Parliament passed an act making forced transportation of criminals legal. In time, however, the colonies objected to having jailbirds dumped on their shores. Female prisoners in particular proved unpopular, and in 1697 England's Council of Trade and Plantations had trouble getting rid of fifty women from Newgate, a notorious prison in London. Massachusetts turned them down and suggested that they be sent to Virginia or Maryland, which had always accepted more indentured servants than the New England colonies. But neither Virginia nor Maryland would take them and they finally ended up on one of the islands of the West Indies.

Settlements that did accept convicts sometimes complained afterward that thefts and other crimes increased. In 1712, South Carolina passed a law to fine any ship's captain who brought criminals of either sex there and also to fine anyone in the colony who tried to obtain such servants. By the mid-1700's, convicts made up only a small portion of the people relocated from the British Isles to North America.

Political prisoners and troublemakers made up the cargoes of some ships. When Charles II died in 1685, the throne of England passed to his brother, who reigned as James II. The Duke of Monmouth, an illegitimate son of Charles II, felt that he had a claim to the throne. Because England had broken with the pope's religious leadership in the 1500's under Henry VIII, Monmouth, a Protestant, easily raised a following against James, who was Catholic. James's forces defeated Monmouth in July, and the duke paid for his rebellion by having his head cut off. His soldiers had little say as to what happened to them, and many soon found themselves on ships headed for the New World, where they became indentured servants. Defeated rebels from various other uprisings during the next half century met a similar fate.

In Ireland and on the Continent, a system of trickery

18

served to gather up laborers. During periods of unemployment, such as the middle and late 1600's, dealers in servants offered work to people who would sign indenture papers. The signers assumed they would be working on estates near their present homes, but when a dealer had enough servants under his control he led them aboard a ship and told them his properties lay across the sea. Only later would they learn that he hadn't actually sailed with them and that they would be turned over to other masters when they reached the colonies. Some dealers insisted that servants who had signed papers of their own free will should receive better treatment aboard ship than convicts or victims of spiriting. They signed agreements to this effect with ship owners. But once the vessel left port, the captain's orders became the only law. A greedy captain could cut down the food rations and in other ways shortchange the passengers. A kind captain would try to live up to his bargain.

No one knows how many adults and youngsters were forcibly removed from Europe. The year 1670 may have been a peak year. At least one historian estimates that during it 10,000 persons were relocated from the British Isles against their will. Some historians wonder if this figure applies to the decade ending with 1670 rather than just to one year, while others doubt that the total number forced to move ever reached such a figure. Starting in 1622, captains were supposed to report the name of every person on their ships, but this regulation was as easily ignored as many of the others. In any case, the number of people who willingly signed indenture papers and came to North America far exceeded the number who had to come against their wishes.

Some of the people spirited to the New World found themselves living far better than they could ever have lived in Europe. Instead of having to starve, steal, or beg, they worked off their debts and became free. Sometimes they were given small acreages of their own, or became regular employees in shops. Many girls found husbands if they wanted to. Their children grew up as respected citizens, even people of influence, such as politicians. Molly Welsh saved any money that came her way and bought a farm of her own after her seven years of service ended.

John Harrower, who came to America of his own free will, was one of the few who left a journal of his period of servitude. In it he included a letter to his family in the British Isles in which he said, "I never lived a genteel regulare life untill now." He also told them that as soon as he finished his period of indenture he intended to make a place "for you all in this Country." Unfortunately, he died before his servitude ended.

Johann Carl Buettner, a young German who traveled rather freely around Europe, fell in with men who pretended to know a ship's captain who would take him to Amsterdam. Once on board ship he found himself a prisoner, along with many other people, and eventually arrived in Philadelphia, to be placed as an indentured servant for six years. His first master traded him to another man in exchange for a team of oxen, after which he wrote in his diary, "I had every reason to be satisfied with my present situation." His worst problem seemed to be homesickness. As a result, when the American Revolution started and the British brought hired Hessian soldiers to the New World, Buettner joined them. When they returned to Germany, he went with them, but thereafter he always referred to himself as Johann Carl Buettner, the American. He did this, he reported, because of spending "my best years in that part of the world" and because he "moistened with my blood the soil of the great North American republic."

20

2
DRAGGED
OUT OF AFRICA
Slave Trade

In August of 1619 a Dutch man-of-war anchored at James-town, Virginia, and offered twenty Africans for sale. They were in a filthy, half-starved condition, even though they reportedly had been aboard the vessel a relatively short time. One rumor said they had been kidnapped from Spanish-held islands in the Caribbean, where slavery had been practiced for years. In such a case, why did they show the effects of a long and unpleasant voyage? It seems more likely, as other reports have stated, that the Dutch vessel had raided a Spanish slave-trading ship somewhere in the Caribbean or off the mainland coast of North America and had taken these blacks as booty. Spain had gained control over Holland in the mid-1500's and did not recognize Dutch independence until a century later. Although a truce existed from 1609 to 1621, Dutchmen and Spaniards clashed when their paths crossed, and Dutch seamen raided Spanish territories and ships at times. The misera-ble blacks on the Dutch vessel probably had been prizes gained during an act of piracy at sea.

The pitiful condition of the blacks on the Dutch ship aroused concern among many people of Jamestown. They thought they could rescue the captives by buying them, which they did. Although they may have saved the lives of those twenty blacks, their "act of mercy" contributed to the death or enslavement of thousands of men, women, and children of Africa who might otherwise have remained free and at peace along the coasts and in the forests of their birth. Dutch, Spanish, Portuguese, and other seamen, assuming that the purchase indicated a market for blacks in mainland North America, in time built up a trade in African slaves. It reached alarming proportions in the next century.

Jamestown, since its founding twelve years earlier, had had a continuous struggle to exist. Its location on a swampy peninsula proved unhealthful and provided poor land for cultivation, but by 1619 some settlers had started plantations on higher, better ground farther up the James River. Indians of the area gave up either their land or their lives rather than serve as indentured servants or slaves. European landholders, as a result, had to use servants brought from Europe or be content with whatever small acreages their own families could cultivate. Because many of them considered themselves above the rugged tasks of clearing and farming land, they gladly accepted indentured servants from the beginning.

Having rescued the blacks from the Dutch ship, the Europeans of Jamestown treated them as indentured servants, requiring them to work for a certain period before giving them their freedom. This became the pattern in British North America during the first half century of settlement. Molly Welsh, who had been forced to relocate in the New World because of trouble over a pail of milk, walked for two days to reach the coast to buy two blacks to help her with the farm she had purchased in Maryland. When they completed their years of indenture with her, she freed them and married one of them. This was probably a rare occurrence. Some historians believe that numbers of white men had black mistresses, whom they might eventually marry or at least treat as wives, but hardly ever did a white woman openly have a black lover or husband.

The fact that she lived inland may have helped Molly escape the disapproval she would undoubtedly have encountered in the growing settlements of the coastal areas. Her husband's name, Bannaky or Bannaka, in time became Banneker, and America's first famous black mathematician and astronomer, Benjamin Banneker, was Molly's grandson.

As settlements in North America increased in number and grew in size, trade with the Caribbean islands and South America became more active. Indentured servitude had given way to slavery on many islands and in Brazil, and colonists on mainland North America soon recognized advantages in having the same servants year after year instead of having to purchase and train new ones from time to time. Massachusetts made slavery legal as early as 1641. In the 1700's plantation owners almost entirely stopped freeing the blacks and children born to the blacks. Slavery became an institution from Massachusetts to Georgia. Although white servants continued to serve their terms of indenture and then go free, blacks saw such rights taken away. Some began to think those of their companions who had died in Africa or on board ship had been lucky.

Perhaps to ease their consciences, slave traders and buyers pointed out that the trade might never have reached large-scale proportions if blacks themselves had not taken an active part in it. If whites had had to hunt the bushes and jungles of Africa to capture slaves, many would have died or become discouraged before obtaining a shipload of humans. But the trinkets, cloth, and rum offered to powerful tribes in exchange for captives encouraged one black group to war on another. As the trade developed, a ship could anchor near a coastal village and soon receive a cargo of prisoners. To speed up the exchange of goods for slaves, trading companies eventually built forts near good anchoring places, and in these the captives could be accumulated and held until a ship arrived. The earliest vessels transporting the victims had been built to carry other types of goods or as armed privateers. The twenty "negars" brought to Jamestown by the Dutch had been carried on the open deck of the ship. But the growth of the trade made captains realize the advantages of designing ships for handling humans by the hundreds rather than in small "batches." By the mid-1700's, the trading pattern had become firmly established.

The trading vessels—sailing from London, Bristol, and Liverpool, England, from Newport, Rhode Island, and from various ports of continental Europe—sought their cargoes along the west coast of Africa. Avoiding the Arab regions of the northern part of Africa's hump, they took their cargoes from what is now Senegal and on south to Angola. Sometimes captains gave chiefs or other officials a taste for rum, after which they promised more liquor in exchange for slaves. Since the officials usually had slaves of their own and assumed that they could easily capture more, they allowed their own servants to be loaded on the ships. If the officials became too drunk to resist, they themselves might regain their senses on board a ship under sail for the New World. Laborers who helped load the vessels might also find themselves held aboard to become part of the slave cargo.

When liquor proved an inadequate tool for acquiring a human cargo, captains spread rumors through a strong tribe that a weaker group planned a raid against it. This stirred the strong tribe to conquer the weak one before such a raid could occur, and the captains filled their holds with the captured innocents. In time, money replaced barter goods, and chiefs, dreaming of things they could buy, sold enemy captives or perhaps some of their own people to obtain the coins. After Europeans erected forts at strategic places along the coast of western Africa, a few whites lived permanently in the forts and continually encouraged strong black hunters to bring in captives.

A European from a fort might even accompany a band

of blacks on a slave-hunting expedition. In canoes, they traveled silently inland from the coast until they sighted a village or smelled smoke or cooking odors from campfires. For the rest of the daylight hours they lay hidden in the bushes at the water's edge, waiting for darkness and full stomachs to make the unsuspecting villagers drowsy. Finally complete silence told the intruders that eating, chores, chatting, lovemaking, and other activities had given way to sleep. The raiders then crept into the camp and took captive the women and children as well as the men, killing those who put up too much resistance. They often set the huts afire to spread confusion among the groggy victims. After binding their quarry with strong twine or ropelike vines, they dragged, carried, or led them to the canoes. Although some villagers escaped, the distance to a friendly settlement usually kept them from summoning help before the canoes headed back to the fort.

Where coasts were swampy, forts had high-walled pens, or barracoons, into which the captors herded the prisoners. The slaves had the damp ground as a floor and the sky as a cover, although some barracoons had roofs of thatch. A corner of each pen might be set aside as a toilet area. The prisoners received water and possibly coconut milk to drink, and tough bread or watery mush and once in a while a little meat, such as monkey, to eat. The only ones who got to leave the enclosures were those responsible for cleaning out the toilet corners once in a while, and they did their chores under a close watch from the Europeans and the warlike blacks who had captured them. Even so, daring victims tried to scale the walls by scrambling up on each other's backs or attempted to break for freedom when they carried the slops outside. Most of them failed, and some lost their lives for their trouble. At least they generally died quickly. Others slowly succumbed to disease, which spread easily in the crowded, unsanitary conditions within the pens. If a ship failed to come soon, only

25

the most hardy remained strong enough to make a last resistance against being forcibly moved to the New World.

Forts built on more solid ground might also have barracoons in which to corral captives, but some had underground dungeons. Here troublemakers could be separated from the more docile victims, who were perhaps tied to trees or stakes near the fort. Or when such a fort was not overcrowded, prisoners could all be placed in the dungeons, allowing their captors to devote less time and effort to standing guard over them. Forts without underground chambers sometimes had ovenlike rooms of stone into which a few troublesome captives could be packed and thereby rendered nearly immobile and helpless. When it came time to load them, the captors bound the men in pairs, one man's left wrist and ankle being shackled to another's right arm and leg. This prevented their bolting for freedom or leaping overboard, and they remained fastened together during the voyage unless one of them died. Women and children had more freedom, but had to provide the sailors with sexual outlets.

In the 1700's some ships designed specifically for carrying slaves sailed the Atlantic. One type had regular holds for cargoes of tobacco, sugar, rum, cotton, cloth, weapons, grain, trinkets, or other goods for which large demands existed, and shallow decks just below the main deck on which the human cargo lay. The space between these half decks and the main one was insufficient to allow a person to stand upright, so captives had to crawl to their places. They spent the six to ten weeks of a voyage lying or crouching, and some captains crowded them in until they lay shoulder to shoulder in rows. Four hundred male prisoners might be packed into an area unsuitable for holding two hundred. Usually no matting softened the planks or protected the men from splinters, and only those wearing loincloths, which provided no warmth, had any covering if the weather grew chilly. Another type of ship had prison decks with room enough for men to stand upright, and in

26

this vessel seven hundred or more men might be lashed to poles. They spent the entire voyage standing groin to groin or groin to buttock and could not find room to sit or lie down even if they worked free of their bonds.

Some captains refrained from overloading their ships, knowing that more of the slaves would probably reach the New World alive and healthy. They received good prices for their captives—upward of fifty pounds per head, or more than double what acquiring, feeding, and transporting the victims had cost. By contrast to these "loose packers," "tight-packing" captains forced prisoners into every available space. They assumed that they made up for loss of life and health among the slaves because of the large numbers of prisoners carried. Even if a third to a half of the captives died and a captain sold the remainder for only thirty-five or forty pounds, he made as much profit as the more humane trader—perhaps more. Slaves who died were thrown into the sea, and packs of sharks reportedly followed some vessels. "Tight-packed" ships reached their destinations in a shroud of stench and yet were welcomed by landowners wanting to cultivate more acres or live in increasing luxury. As commerce in white indentured servants decreased in the 1700's, trade in black slaves increased.

Some ports had regular buildings in which slaves stood for auction like horses or cattle. After a landowner or businessman purchased the captives he wanted, he tied them by ropes to his buggy and led them home or placed them in a wagon for the trip. A few might be trained to work in the house and, particularly in town, might even live in a part of the house set aside for servants. Most worked on the land and occupied small wooden huts some distance from the master's dwelling. For a while they might be kept shackled until they showed a willingness to settle down to their new lives, but even so some escaped to live with Indians, to die of exposure or starvation, or to pass as free men if they reached settlements where they were unknown and where free blacks were beginning to congregate.

Just as thoughtful people became disturbed about spiriting and turning white captives into indentured servants, a few recognized the horrors and unfairness of dealing in black slaves. They particularly became upset by the trade when the advantages of it began to decline. Partly for this reason, in Massachusetts and other northern colonies where growing populations made small farms rather than huge estates practical, antislavery feelings gradually became strong. There were, of course, those women and men in the South as well as in the North who had always disapproved of one person's claiming to own another. As new voices joined theirs, the call for abolishing slavery could be heard throughout the colonies.

When colonial governments refused to abolish slave trade, some cities, such as Boston and Salem, sought permission to outlaw slavery within their own limits. But it took the outbreak of the American Revolution to make great numbers of people fully conscious of the unfair double standard in the New World. As they fought for freedom from unfair treatment by the British, some Revolutionaries began to see the parallel of their own unfair treatment of blacks. If they felt that one country had no legal right to hold another in bondage, how could they believe that one human being had the right to hold another? Virginia and Maryland did not outlaw slavery, but during the war they made it illegal for slaves to be brought in for sale. Massachusetts and Pennsylvania passed laws that not only stopped the trade but also in time freed the blacks within those regions. After the war, New Jersey stopped the importation of slaves, and North Carolina started putting impossibly high duties on them. South Carolina at times stopped the importation of slaves, yet when the infant federal government wanted to outlaw the slave trade in the newly formed United States of America, South Carolina, along with Georgia, threatened to withdraw from the federation. Gradually the sides were drawn up that would eventually fight the Civil War.

Some Africans proved docile about relocation, but most had to be subdued and some never willingly surrendered to being moved. Captain Thomas Phillips of the slave ship *Hannibal*, sailing in 1693, reported, "The negroes are so wilful and loth to leave their country, that they have often leap'd out of the canoos, boat and ship, into the sea, and kept under water till they were drowned, to avoid being taken up and saved by our boats, which pursued them; they have a more dreadful apprehension of Barbadoes than we can have of hell. . . . We had about twelve negroes did wilfully drown themselves, and others starv'd themselves to death; for 'tis their belief that when they die they return home to their own country and friends again."

After having been brought to the New World and sold into slavery, one man took the name Charles Ball, under which the story of his enslavement was told. "About twenty persons were seized in our village at the time I was; and amongst these were three children so young that they were not able to walk. . . . When they put us in irons . . . the men who fastened the irons on these mothers took the children out of their hands and threw them over the side of the ship into the water. When this was done, two of the women leaped overboard after the children—the third was already confined by a chain to another woman and could not get into the water, but in struggling to disengage herself, she broke her arm and died a few days after of a fever. One of the two women who were in the river was carried down by the weight of her irons before she could be rescued, but the other was taken up by some men in a boat and brought on board. This woman threw herself overboard one night when we were at sea."

3
PUSHED
BACK
Eastern Indians

When the English colonists who were sent to America by the Virginia Company of London founded Jamestown in 1607, they knew little of farming. They settled on a swampy neck of land about thirty miles up a river they called the James in honor of their king, James I. The time, mid-May, though somewhat late, was satisfactory for planting seeds, but in the poor soil of the peninsula the newcomers found it difficult to grow crops. Since many of the first settlers considered themselves gentlemen—above the ranks of laborers and farmers—they rarely stooped to hoeing out the weeds that competed with the food-producing plants. Between the poor soil and the lack of energy devoted to tilling it, they guaranteed trouble for themselves.

Along the banks of the river lived naked or nearly naked people with tan to reddish-brown skins. Christopher Columbus, who first took word of the New World and its tribes back to Europe, had called these people Indians, thinking he had reached India. Later explorers often referred to them as "beasts," "animals," and "infidels," terms that the English settlers accepted without question. But these "ignorant" and "pagan" Indians managed to grow the grain and vegetables they needed for survival.

During its first winters, Jamestown continued in existence only because the Indians shared their produce and the prizes of their hunting expeditions with the colonists.

Even the worst white farmer eventually realized that the land occupied by the Indians must be better for food production than the low-lying peninsula. The leaders of Jamestown bought some land along the banks of the James, and the settlers finally managed to raise a surplus to help them through the cold months. To raise still larger crops, they planted seeds on more and more land, as though their initial purchases entitled them to whatever ground they wanted to occupy. The puzzled Indians moved back into the forests and up the river. Summer after summer the white colonists pushed forward and the Indians retreated. Young braves grew angry, but their chief, Powhatan, counseled them to remain at peace with the newcomers. He hoped to reach an understanding through talks, and reminded the whites of the kind treatment they had received from the Indians. Why, he asked, did they take the land and the food of the Indian people by force when the Indians, during the cold winters, had proved they would peacefully share what they had? The whites explained that God intended for Christians to control the land and to convert the "infidel" from his heathen ways.

This made little sense to most Indians. Neither, for that matter, did the sale of land. Indians understood the exchange of a fox skin for a gun, a keg of rum, or even a few colorful trinkets. One person handed over an object and received an object or objects in return. But the land stretched away endlessly. It could no more be handed by one person to another than could the sunshine. The lands were part of creation. They existed for all. When the Indians first "sold" land to the colonists, they really meant that they gave the whites the privilege of sharing it with them. But the white man put up rail fences and behaved like a wolf protecting its den and cubs.

31

Powhatan died, and the chief who followed him frowned at the white man's behavior. The settlers, still thinking they acted with God's favor, failed to realize how much of a change a new chief could mean. Particularly did the missionaries who had come to Jamestown ignore the signs of trouble. About fifty of these ministers had arrived, and they grew discouraged at trying to convert adult Indians to Christianity. Although they had won the minds of a few, they decided they could make more rapid progress if they concentrated on the children. But the adult Indians who objected to giving up their own beliefs had no intention of letting their children be converted. Considering that they acted for the benefit of the youngsters, the ministers had them kidnapped and taken to Jamestown for schooling. The new chief gave the word for war, to recover the land as much as to recover the children. Braves devastated the plantations, murdering the people along the way as they headed for Jamestown. An Indian who had accepted Christianity raced ahead of the warriors and reached the stockade in time to warn of the danger. Bolting the gates, the settlers inside the walls fought off the Indians, but in that massacre of 1622 about 350 whites lost their lives.

By the time of the Jamestown massacre, a second permanent English settlement had been made in what was to become the United States. A group of Separatists—people unwilling to accept the teachings and practices of the Church of England—hoped to free themselves of European influences by settling in the New World. Accompanied by other discontented families, these Pilgrims anchored the *Mayflower* off Plymouth Rock in December 1620. They had known hard work before. Unlike the first settlers of Jamestown, they expected to have to struggle. And they obviously would have to wait for spring before they tilled the soil and planted seeds. The ship served as their home until a settlement could be established.

On their fourth day in the New World, some of the

Pilgrims saw half a dozen Indians and a dog approaching. The "savages," on seeing the Pilgrims, "ran into the Woods and whistled the Dogge after them." Had the Pilgrims remained calm and waited for the curiosity of the Indians to draw them out of the forest, they might have established friendly contact on that day. Instead, the whites gave chase, possibly making enough noise to sound like an army. The Indians easily outdistanced the newcomers, without crashing and thrashing through the underbrush to mark the trail of their escape. Perhaps the pursuit by the whites made the Indians suspect them of being unfriendly. When a larger band of Indians returned a few days later, they sent "their arrowes . . . flying amongst us" from behind the protection of trees. The whites fired back with muskets until the Indian leader gave a wild cry and all the attackers fled away through the forest. Injuries on both sides were light.

The meager supplies on the *Mayflower* and the game they hunted in the forest kept the Pilgrims alive during the first weeks. Both night and day they kept a close watch for attackers, but their next encounter with Indians proved friendly. A lesser chief, Samoset, came alone and, to their surprise, spoke to them in English, which he had learned from fishermen and traders who had visited the northeast coast off and on for a number of years. He told them that a great chief called Massasoit headed the Wampanoag groups of the area. These had once numbered many people, but a terrible disease—probably smallpox—had recently spread through the tribes and had killed more than it had spared. This explained why the surrounding territory seemed to be deserted. With the help of the Indians, the settlers survived the winter. In time, Massasoit paid the settlers a visit himself. During his stay in Plymouth, as the Pilgrims named the settlement, the chief and Governor William Bradford agreed on a treaty of peace and drank "strong water" to seal it.

The leaders at Plymouth established a colonial court to

33

handle disputes and land agreements. When a settler in good standing in the colony desired a piece of land, the court often awarded it to him on condition that he pay the Indian owners for it. The wishes of the Indians made little difference. If they resisted occupation of the land, the settlers drove them off and claimed possession without paying. The Indians learned that they fared better when they accepted knives, kettles, foodstuffs, clothing, "strong water," and trinkets in exchange for the land than when they tried to hold back the encroachments of the newcomers. Certain lesser chiefs wanted to go to war, but Massasoit honored the treaty of peace he had made and held the leaders under him in check. Other Europeans seeking freedom of worship, along with adventurers wanting to leave England, settled near Plymouth during the next few decades. In time, these groups became the colony of Massachusetts. As long as he lived, Massasoit kept his bargain of peace with the settlers at Plymouth and with the other villages that sprang up in his territory.

Massasoit died in 1661, having lived about eighty years, a long life for a white or an Indian in those days of famine, little-understood diseases, and few medicines. The oldest son survived Massasoit by less than a year, which brought the second son, Metacomet (Pometacom), to the leadership of the Wampanoag Indians. Metacomet, better known today as King Philip, drank "strong water" with the settlers and agreed to the treaties honored by his father. But he lacked his father's calm in the face of European advances into farming and hunting areas. He let his subordinates arm themselves as though for war. Alarmed, the Europeans called Philip to a meeting at Taunton to explain such conduct, but for a time he refused to go. When he did, in 1671, the officials at Taunton fined him and demanded that he and his followers give up some of the muskets they had acquired over the years. Philip surrendered his at the time, as did the few lesser chiefs with him, and promised to send the weapons of his warriors as soon as he returned to where they awaited him. But by this time he had learned to break promises, which he felt the whites had done with him. Once outside Taunton, he rearmed himself and led his warriors away.

During the next few years, Philip arranged for support from the Narragansett of Rhode Island and the Nipmuck of western Massachusetts. All were under pressure from the expanding colony and felt the necessity of war to protect their rights. They probably intended to launch it in 1676. Preaching Christianity among the tribes, a Wampanoag Indian called Sassamon acted as an informer to the Europeans. In 1673 or 1674, he left his ministry and hurried to Plymouth to report news of the war preparations. Indians faithful to Philip learned of Sassamon's act, which by Indian law made him subject to a death penalty. Probably on Philip's orders, braves went in search of the traitor, and in January 1675 he was last seen alive by white men. That spring, as the ice melted, his body was discovered at the bottom of a shallow lake. Rumors quickly spread that he had committed suicide by drowning himself, a suitable end for a spy, but the colonists could not be fooled. Marks on Sassamon's body and a broken neck indicated that he had been beaten to death before being shoved through a hole in the ice. Three Indians had been seen in the vicinity of Assowamsett Pond, as the lake was called, and the settlers arrested them. According to one wild report, blood oozed from the wounds on Sassamon's corpse when each of these three men was brought to view it. In any case, a jury of twelve colonists and six Indians found the three guilty; two were hanged and one was shot.

Without waiting for Philip to give the signal, some warriors under his command openly went on the warpath, starting the war ahead of schedule. This cost the Indians the element of surprise in addition to forcing them to fight before preparations had been completed. The Narragansett, refusing to be rushed into battle, held back until they could better ready themselves for war. Left unsupported

35

from the south, the Wampanoag had little chance of wiping out the European settlements. By the time the Narragansett joined King Philip's War, the Wampanoag had already been considerably weakened. Between the execution of the three suspected killers of Sassamon in June 1675 and the killing of Philip in August 1676, Massachusetts and Rhode Island saw some of the bloodiest massacres and reprisals ever to occur on American soil. The fierce Nipmuck completely destroyed more than a dozen western villages, burning the buildings and slaughtering the settlers. The Narragansett had less success and were nearly all killed. With them eliminated by early 1676, the colonial militia went in support of settlers in western Massachusetts and subdued the Nipmuck within months.

Philip and the Wampanoag continued the fight. Avoiding open warfare, as was customary among woodland Indians, they struck from ambush and made sudden rushes upon settlements, attacking by night or day as conditions seemed to favor them. But the foreigners had by now adopted the Indian method of fighting and also used ambushes and surprise attacks to good advantage. Besides, after a setback or a victory the Europeans often swept forward for further combat, while the Indians often took time out to rest or celebrate and unexpectedly found themselves fighting again before they were ready. Philip finally sought a hiding place in a Rhode Island swamp, but one of his followers slipped away and took word of his whereabouts to the English. In the surprise attack that followed, an Indian fighting with the settlers shot Philip and the war ended for lack of his leadership.

Forced relocation for Indians could mean more than being pushed off the lands they farmed and hunted. In some regions it even meant being kidnapped, for sale as slaves. The Tuscarora of North Carolina faced this situation. White settlers from Virginia pushed into North Carolina as early as the 1650's, and other groups of settlers came from England. Like early colonists elsewhere, those

36

who first came to North Carolina sometimes had difficulty in producing or finding enough food for survival during the winters. According to a surveyor, John Lawson, the Tuscarora Indians always "freely gave us of their victuals." But though the Tuscarora might be starving on occasion, the new settlers generally ignored them.

If a healthy-looking Indian boy or girl went to a cabin to ask for food, the youngster might be captured, sent elsewhere, and sold as a slave. Although many Indians starved rather than serve in bondage, the Tuscarora could be made to work. As a result, a trade in Tuscarora Indians grew until warriors of the tribe attacked isolated cabins in retaliation. After that the Indian slave trade increased or dropped off as the settlers grew bold or frightened.

In 1710 a group of Swiss and Germans came to North Carolina seeking land for a settlement. The leader, Baron Christopher von Graffenreid, had no knowledge of treaty arrangements and fell victim of a trick. Some Englishmen, who didn't altogether welcome the German-speaking newcomers, sold him land belonging to the Tuscarora, telling him it was unoccupied. Why the Indians allowed the Europeans to build a settlement is unclear. Perhaps they tried to reason with the intruders, or turned to the colonial government for support under the provisions of existing treaties. Whatever the Indians did, the Swiss and Germans proceeded with their plans, naming their settlement New Berne, after the city of Berne, Switzerland. At the same time, the slave kidnappers became active once more, perhaps hoping that the latest arrivals from Europe would receive the blame.

The Tuscarora suddenly attacked New Berne and killed seventy of the inhabitants. Aid for the whites came from Virginia and South Carolina as well as from the surrounding area, and the Tuscarora wars began, lasting more than a year. Von Graffenreid, when taken prisoner by the Indians, promised them ammunition, liquor, and his neutrality if they let him go, which they did. He kept part of the bargain, but when the colonists appeared to be winning he joined them in an effort to defeat the Tuscarora. Some Indian tribes of the region sided with the whites. In the final major battle, the Tuscarora occupied a fort and faced only about three dozen whites. But the colonists had the support of nearly nine hundred Indians, mainly from the Cherokee and Catawba tribes. Short on ammunition and supplies, the Tuscarora met a defeat so disastrous that it ended their ability as well as their will to fight. As after other Indian defeats, many of the remaining Tuscarora were sold into slavery.

In the early spring of 1713, the Tuscarora survivors started moving north to join the Iroquois tribes, to which they were related. They generally moved in small bands, causing uneasiness along their route as they went. The last of them may not have left North Carolina until the first decade of the 1800's. Some settled in Pennsylvania, but others went on to the Finger Lakes area of New York to be with the five tribes of the Iroquois confederacy—the Cayuga, Mohawk, Oneida, Onondaga, and Seneca. Not all their northern relatives welcomed them, but the Oneida supported them in the league and won them a membership of sorts, although they lacked voting privileges.

During the American Revolution the Tuscarora split into two factions—those who supported the British and those who aided the colonists. The Iroquois league itself split. This helps to explain why the Indians throughout North and South America lost their lands to invaders. Some acted as spies or became turncoats. Unfortunately, they proved to be generous and trusting at the wrong times. They gave a mile when they shouldn't have given an inch. A simple way of life had hardly prepared them for dealing with more sophisticated peoples. It is easy for us to see these things today, yet we don't seem to be in any hurry to reexamine some of the old treaties that may still be in effect. These don't necessarily date from colonial times, before the American Revolution. They include agreements drawn up by a free and independent United States Government.

One of the major spokesmen for the Indians following the formation of an independent United States of America was Tecumseh, leader of the Shawnee. With a sense of history seldom credited to the Indians by whites, he cried, "Where today are the Pequot? Where are the Narragansett, the Mohican, the Pokanoket, and many other once powerful tribes of our people? They have vanished before . . . the oppression of the White Man, as snow before a summer sun. Will we let ourselves be destroyed in our turn without a struggle, give up our homes, our country bequeathed to us by the Great Spirit . . . and everything that is dear and sacred to us?"

He saw the War of 1812 as a chance for the Indians to stop the westward push of land-hungry whites. As a result, Tecumseh advised joining the British, even though it had been the British who destroyed the Narragansett and some of the other tribes whose passing he lamented. Pushmataha, leader of the Choctaw, took a different view. He advised, "Be not deceived with illusive hopes. . . . Listen to the voice of prudence, ere you rashly act. But do as you may. . . . I shall join our friends, the Americans, in this war."

When General Henry A. Proctor, with whom Tecumseh fought, planned a retreat after a defeat at the hands of American forces, Tecumseh tried to change his mind. Failing in this, Tecumseh reportedly asked for arms and ammunition so that the Indians could continue the fight. "Our lives are in the hands of the Great Spirit," Tecumseh told Proctor. "We are determined to defend our lands, and if it be his will, we wish to leave our bones upon them." But Proctor was concerned about the British, not about the Indians. Soon after, Tecumseh was killed in battle.

4
TO
THE DEFEATED
The Acadians

The Canadian region known to the English as Acadia (the French called it Acadie) had vague boundaries. To the Micmac Indians, from whose language the word probably comes, it consisted of the land they occupied between the mouth of the St. Lawrence River and the Atlantic Ocean, roughly what is now Nova Scotia and northern New Brunswick. In the first decade of the 1600's, the French attempted to establish settlements on islands off the coast of Maine and along the coast of Nova Scotia. These generally lasted only short periods but gave France its claim to the Micmac region. By the 1620's, a handful of French colonists and fur traders had become permanently established. England also claimed the area and, after the late 1620's, troubled the French repeatedly. The French position should have been the stronger during the 1600's because of a larger and growing French population, but civil war between French leaders in the area and long periods during which France gave no assistance to the colony kept it weak. By the end of the 1600's, the French, called Acadians by the English, occupied mainly Nova Scotia, the St. John Valley of New Brunswick, and northern Maine.

England finally gained control of Nova Scotia in the early 1700's. France, realizing that it might be squeezed out of that part of North America altogether, started settlements and built forts in nearby regions, especially on Cape Breton Island, which later became part of Nova Scotia. Some French colonists migrated to different sections of New Brunswick and to Île-St-Jean (now Prince Edward Island). Others joined the French already living in areas that are now eastern Quebec and northern Maine. It worried the British colonists of Boston and other parts of New England to have the Acadians so near and becoming more numerous. Europe's political conflicts involving France and England spilled over into the New World, resulting in raids from Acadia into New England and from New England into Acadia. Even when peace existed in Europe, skirmishes occurred in North America. These local encounters often had more to do with economics than with politics, but that made them no less disturbing. Acadian fishing vessels competed with those of New England in the fishing areas off the coasts of New England, Nova Scotia, and Newfoundland, keeping alive ill feelings. And with lumbering so important during the days of wooden ships and buildings, the Maine forests looked like riches to both the Acadians and the New Englanders.

The Indians provided other major reasons for conflict between the French and the English in Acadia. When settling in the Micmac region, the French generally proved willing to live side by side with the Indians. Except for converting the Indians to Catholicism, the Acadians allowed them to continue in most of their old ways. Instead of taking over Micmac lands already prepared for agriculture, the French cleared land of their own. When doing so, they left enough forest areas to provide the Indians and themselves with hunting grounds. Many young men came from France without wives or sweethearts and they married Indian women or lived with them as though in marriage, building up family ties between themselves and the Micmac which they willingly acknowledged. The British, by contrast, sometimes attempted to take over

41

whatever land they wanted, paying little attention to Indian or French claims. This crowded some Micmac and Acadians out of their hunting and farming areas, leading to murders and to the burning of English cabins. English farmers occasionally took Indian wives or lovers, but when the men visited friends or an English settlement they might leave the women at home as though ashamed of them. Some Indian women must have felt more like slaves than wives. In raising his children, the Englishman might treat them strictly as Indians or he might try to make them fully British, but he seldom seemed to see himself as belonging in two worlds—the Indian and the foreign. In those days, many of the English had strong antipapal prejudices and therefore distrusted all Catholics, French or Indian.

Because of the different way in which the French lived in association with the Micmac, they usually remained at peace with them whereas the English had trouble. The English sometimes suspected the French of stirring up conflict, and certainly blamed them for remaining neutral when the English needed help. In addition, the Indians at times crossed the farms or passed through the villages of the Acadians on their way to raid English farms and settlements. When the British asked for the identities of the raiders or called on the Acadians to give warnings of raids to come, the French gave no assistance. Yet the Acadians might alert the Indians to a British attack. Understandably, the British considered both the Acadians and the Indians as enemies.

Europe's War of the Austrian Succession became known as King George's War in North America because George II held the British throne at the time. After fighting ended in 1748, the British soon built a headquarters at Halifax, Nova Scotia, so they could keep an eye on the French. New England colonists pressured the leaders to drive the Acadians out, but at first the major aim seemed to be to maintain peace. In time the British tried to make the French swear loyalty to the king of England, which the Acadians refused to do without a guarantee that they would not have to fight for England in case of war. The British could not, or would not, give any such promise. Foreseeing repeated conflicts if the French remained, the British leader Charles Lawrence, without consulting his superiors in London, finally decided that the Acadians had to be removed.

On July 28, 1755, the British administration in Halifax announced its plan to distribute the Acadians throughout the colonies farther south. Many of the people of French descent looked on this as a new trick to frighten them into taking an oath of allegiance to King George, but in a matter of days British soldiers pounded on their doors and took the men prisoner. At Grand Pré, Nova Scotia, British officers assembled the men at the church and held them until they could be loaded onto vessels in the harbor. In some places the Acadians had so little warning that they found themselves being herded to the ships without a chance to save belongings other than the clothes they wore. Men working their fields might be dragged off to jail and eventually to a ship with no opportunity to say goodby to their families. Where a family barricaded itself in its cabin and refused to surrender to the British troops, the soldiers burned the house down and captured the people as the flames drove them out. Men who refused to be subdued might be killed. A surprising number of Acadians went peacefully, just as they had remained at peace when British and Indian wars surged about their farms and fishing villages.

Perhaps at first Governor Lawrence intended to deport just the men—the earliest shiploads contained only male passengers. But some Acadian women didn't sit idly by. They attacked the British soldiers with their husbands' guns and with whatever they could use as clubs in attempts to rescue their men. They called on the Indians for help, which they sometimes received. It quickly became obvious that removing just the men would fail to eliminate French-English friction in Acadia. As a result, orders went out from Halifax for women and children to be deported as well as men. The soldiers made no effort to keep families together. At times they probably separated relatives intentionally, especially if a family proved particularly difficult to manage.

Some Acadians fled to the forests and lived in hiding or with the Indians, although the British tried to hunt them down. Others migrated to Quebec and French-held areas farther inland, such as the Ohio River valley, and a few managed to find passage on ships sailing for France. At first the removal concentrated on Nova Scotia, but soon it spread to New Brunswick. It continued until the beginning of the 1760's, with Prince Edward Island becoming a target for removals in 1758. Reports vary on how many Acadians had to move. It may have been six thousand, or it may have been more than ten thousand. Perhaps two to four thousand Acadians were allowed to stay on their land and in their villages. These people remained neutral, even when the Seven Years' War broke out between the French and the English in 1756 to determine who would control North America.

Governor Lawrence expected New Englanders to flock north in their eagerness to settle on the vacated lands of the Acadians. After all, part of the reason for shipping away the settlers of French descent was to satisfy complaints about them from the New England colonies, especially Massachusetts. Lawrence circulated reports of the abundant acres of farm and orchard land to the south and indicated these would be given out generously. But only a trickle of New Englanders came north, and another trickle of new settlers came from the British Isles. The British then welcomed Protestants from Germany, Switzerland, and other parts of continental Europe, for they probably would side against the Catholic French if forced into a conflict. Indians occupied some of the farms, but the

44

rest lay idle until peace returned after the British victory in 1763. Discharged British soldiers settled on some of the farms, although in general they made poor farmers and moved away after failing to prosper.

In the colonies farther south, the deported Acadians found a chilly welcome at best and open antagonism in many places. Labor shortages no longer hampered the American colonists as badly as in earlier years, and even where workers were needed, the colonists wanted indentured servants or slaves rather than free men who would expect decent wages. Since they were scattered through all the colonies from Maine to South Carolina, the Acadians usually formed groups too small to build settlements of their own in which they could retain their old customs and live independently of their neighbors. There might be no land available where they found themselves, and many had no money to buy even when there was. They gradually adopted the ways of the people among whom they had to resettle, although they clung to their Catholic faith. Numbers of the Acadians tried to make their way to New Orleans or to the Ohio Valley to be with other people of French descent. And some no sooner landed in an unfriendly port than they started seeking ways to return to the maritime regions of Canada. Small groups of them did manage to return, but they lived in fear until peace came in 1763. They also lived under severe hardships, for they often found their old farm buildings burned or else occupied by new settlers. They couldn't be too active in establishing new claims, because they might attract attention to themselves and bring on a second removal.

After England won the Seven Years' War, the British allowed Acadians to return openly to their old regions if they swore allegiance to England. Following the disheartening ordeal of the removal and without their old leaders and priests, who had been firmly against their taking such an oath, most of those who wanted to return agreed to the British demands. A few found their lands awaiting them,

45

but most had to make a new start. Perhaps two thousand eventually found their way home and faced the struggle of building cabins and clearing land to begin again. With European Protestants, New Englanders, and former British soldiers for neighbors as often as not, they did not return to their old ways. In time their descendants usually felt more loyalty to the province in which they lived than to their Acadian background.

Almost a century after the removal started, Henry Wadsworth Longfellow recognized the terrible episode as material for a romantic tragedy. In *Evangeline: A Tale of Acadie*, the poet has Evangeline Bellefontaine separated from Gabriel Lajeunesse, the man to whom she has just become engaged.

> There disorder prevailed, and the tumult and stir of embarking.
> Busily plied the freighted boats; and in the confusion
> Wives were torn from their husbands, and mothers, too late, saw their children
> Left on the land, extending their arms, with wildest entreaties.
> So unto separate ships were Basil and Gabriel carried,
> While in despair on the shore Evangeline stood with her father.

They are resettled in different places, but Evangeline wanders in search of Gabriel, just as many Acadians really did seek to find the loved ones from whom they had been parted accidentally or by design.

> Far asunder, on separate coasts, the Acadians landed;
> Scattered were they, like flakes of snow, when the wind from the northeast
> Strikes aslant through the fogs that darken the Banks of Newfoundland.
> Friendless, homeless, hopeless, they wandered from city to city,
> From the cold lakes of the North to sultry Southern savannas,—

46

From the bleak shores of the sea to the lands where the Father
      of Waters
Seizes the hills in his hands, and drags them down to the
      ocean,
Deep in their sands to bury the scattered bones of the mam-
      moth.
Friends they sought and homes; and many, despairing, heart-
      broken,
Asked of the earth but a grave, and no longer a friend nor a
      fireside.

Evangeline eventually finds the farm where Gabriel has
been living, but he has left and her search must continue.
Only in old age, when Gabriel is dying in poverty, do they
finally meet again. They are buried in unmarked graves in
a noisy city far from the quiet fields they had known in
Acadia.

Based on actual events, Longfellow's narrative poem
has played an important part in keeping people of Canada
and the United States reminded of a sad episode.

5
BACK
TO AFRICA
Liberia

By the time the American Revolution ended, numbers of free blacks roamed city streets or country roads seeking work, or they lived on small acreages from which they often reaped less food than their families needed. In periods of desperation, they stole from whoever had more, usually the whites. This had more to do with survival than racial conflict, but it frightened property owners. Especially when a white person got injured, killed, or raped during what started out to be a robbery, communities trembled for fear of a racial revolution.

In the South, plantation holders often had more slaves than they wanted. What could a master do with blacks grown too old to work? If these people went free, they had no way of earning a living, yet thoughtless and uncaring owners turned them loose to beg, live at the mercy of relatives, or steal. More kindly masters kept them on the plantation, providing them with necessities but little more. In some cases, the elderly looked after the growing numbers of babies and children, leaving the in-between group to be the servants and laborers.

Whites resented or feared able-bodied blacks of working age who had paid for their freedom or had gained it by some other means. Some of these freedmen had a natural ability to lead and could have stirred the slaves to revolt. All of them, simply by taking jobs and working for wages, made the people who were still in bondage discontent with a slave's life. Legislators and other influential persons began to seek ways to get rid of those blacks whose presence seemed to be a social or an economic threat. Great Britain faced a somewhat similar problem and worked out what appeared to be a solution.

The British Isles never became a major slaveholding region. But during the American Revolution, British soldiers and sailors often kidnapped blacks or helped them escape from the rebellious colonies, transporting them to Nova Scotia or to Great Britain. Some of the British felt they did a humane act by carrying blacks to freedom, while others hoped to weaken the colonies by taking away part of the labor force. After the war England did not want the former slaves and decided to take them back to Africa. Even before the war, a few people had suggested doing this, but only after the fighting had ceased did officials and slaveholders give it serious thought. After England founded a colony for free Negroes in Sierra Leone in 1787, Americans slowly formed plans for a similar settlement.

In 1800 politicians in Virginia asked their governor, James Monroe, to contact President John Adams about buying foreign land for a black colony. Other states took the idea seriously as time passed, until by 1816 concerned people really desired action. A New Jersey pastor, Robert Finley, with President James Madison's backing, called for a meeting in Washington in December to set up the machinery for establishing a black colony. Under Henry Clay's chairmanship, the members formed the American Society for Colonizing the Free People of Color of the United States. Bushrod Washington, nephew of America's first president, became head of the society on the first day of January 1817. The second article of the organization's constitution stated that the resettlement program would be carried out "with their consent," that is, with the consent of the blacks involved. With this objective, the society should have been safe from accusations of forcing people to move against their will, but such was not the case.

During the society's first few years, its work amounted to meeting and talking, meeting and talking. Bushrod Washington, although a capable justice of the Supreme Court, lacked the drive of his famous uncle. Besides, he and other leaders of the society had little interest in making the colonization plan work if the finances for it had to come out of their own purses. Individual states were supposed to handle their own efforts at finding land, acquiring settlement rights, and transporting free blacks to it, but their legislators failed to vote the money needed. Finally the United States Government began to take a strong interest in the resettlement idea.

After Congress appropriated $100,000 to assist the colonization society, a group of some eighty free blacks voluntarily, as far as we know, sailed on the schooner *Elizabeth* early in 1820. The ship landed its passengers at Sherbro Island, off the coast of Sierra Leone, where another shipload of free blacks joined them a year later. But these Negroes lacked immunity to African diseases. Nearly a third of the group died, along with Samuel Bacon, the white minister in charge of helping them get settled. The survivors fled to Sierra Leone, where the British had already faced the problems of local fevers and could provide some degree of medical protection.

In 1822, Captain R. F. Stockton sailed to Africa with a load of blacks rescued from slave-trading ships and decided that Cape Mesurado (Montserado), near the mouth of the Mesurado River, provided a safe anchoring place. The tribes already living there proved unfriendly, but Stockton talked them into signing treaties. Warlike acts occurring later indicate that the local chiefs probably decided to pretend agreement in order to capture the new settlers and sell them as slaves as soon as Stockton removed his warship from the area. The colony was immediately strengthened, however, when the American slaves that had gone from Sherbro Island to Sierra Leone were brought the relatively short distance to the Mesurado River, renamed the St. Paul. With them came a white doctor and a dynamic Negro leader, Elijah Johnson. With the doctor to fight disease and Johnson to fight the local tribes and slave captains, the new colony managed to survive. In time it took the name Liberia, from the Latin word *liber*, meaning "free," while the settlement was called Monrovia to honor America's president, James Monroe.

Disease and fighting kept the original colony from growing strong. But the fact that it existed at all gave the colonization society courage to make additional settlements. In 1834, Maryland shipped a group of free blacks, who landed at Cape Palmas near the Cavally River. Virginia sent more than a hundred former slaves from one plantation, after the owner's death freed them. They settled between Monrovia and Cape Palmas, on the Grain Coast, so named because it produced a grain from which a popular pepper came. And the Young Men's Colonization Society of Pennsylvania sent over yet another group. All these small settlements had to fight with the local tribes to escape enslavement and to compete with one another for trade in order to live above a subsistence level. A Negro leader, Thomas Buchanan, recognized the necessity of eliminating jealousies and encouraging cooperation among the settlements strung along the Grain Coast. He called for a meeting of leaders, who drew up agreements that would bring all the settlements together as one colony. The Liberia formed in this way had its western boundary about a hundred miles west of Monrovia, where the Morro River provided a natural border with Sierra Leone. The Cavally River separated Liberia from the Ivory Coast on the east. Although the original settlement had claimed land for only two miles inland from the shore, the nation eventually extended inland for about 150 miles in places. In spite of a coastline of 350 miles, the colony lacked good harbors and attracted fewer trading vessels than some of the neighboring regions.

Reports of Liberia's troubles with fevers, warlike tribes, an uncomfortable climate, meager trade, and a lack of financial support from Washington reached the United States. These reports hardly encouraged large numbers of free blacks to want to migrate. By the mid-1840's, only about five thousand blacks had gone to Liberia to settle. A handful of them controlled the government and wrote the laws for the others and for possibly 200,000 local people, who continued their tribal existence with little concern about the constitution drawn up on the pattern of that of the United States. The government in Washington reserved the right to veto legislation of the Liberian Congress, but in general it allowed the colony to rule itself. After Buchanan died and his subordinate, Joseph J. Roberts, became governor, leaders began to think the colony's troubles might be solved through independence. This stand had a degree of logic, for nations of Europe sometimes refused to recognize Liberia's right to impose trading duties and in other ways try to raise funds. Roberts, a colored man with white blood in his veins, declared the land's independence in 1847 and took control as the new nation's first president. In becoming independent, Liberia not only separated itself from the United States but also broke with the American Colonization Society, a name adopted in 1837. The society continued to support migration to Liberia, however, especially after the Emancipation Proclamation and the Civil War freed all blacks in the United States.

If a slave owner provided for his blacks to go free when he died, they might never have a chance to learn what freedom in the United States could mean. A representative for the society either talked them into going to Liberia or let them think they had no choice in the matter. Or perhaps he let them think the ship they sailed on would take them to New York or Boston when in reality its destination was Africa. Plantation masters sometimes said certain blacks had agreed to go when such was far from the truth. In this way, the owners shipped off Negroes too old to work and younger ones who stirred up trouble. In the North as well as the South, some blacks who had been arrested went from prison to a ship and sailed for Liberia without knowing where they would land and without a chance to have their objections heard. And there existed cases of outright kidnapping.

Not all white people stood quietly by and allowed the exiling of blacks to take place. William Lloyd Garrison fiercely opposed slavery and in time gained recognition as the leading abolitionist in the United States. At first, according to his book *Thoughts on African Colonization,* he supported the American Colonization Society. As he read its annual *Report* and its paper, the *African Repository,* he came to doubt the value and sincerity of the group's work. By the early 1830's he came to oppose the society as heatedly as he did the institution of slavery, after discovering what he called the group's "sinful palliations, fatal concessions, vain expectations, exaggerated statements, unfriendly representations, glaring contradictions, naked terrors, deceptive assurances, unrelenting prejudices, and unchristian denunciations." To learn the black citizen's point of view, he talked with free people of color in the streets and addressed their gatherings. Soon he reported that free blacks "almost *unanimously* opposed . . . removal," and later he said, "I have never seen one of their number who was friendly to this scheme."

Garrison said the society promised blacks great improvements in their living conditions if they went to Africa but stood in the way of their achieving improvements as long as they stayed in the United States. Actually, the blacks had to live in thatch huts in Liberia and needed to clear jungle growth from the land before planting so much as a garden. Garrison said the society failed to keep its promises, especially when it advertised that it placed the free blacks "where no obstacles will impede their march to affluence, preferment and honor." One of the aims of the colonization society was to Christianize Africa. As Garrison pointed out, this required leaders properly educated for the work and not the relocated people who lacked training as missionaries. Faced with the old pagan beliefs of Africa, they would be as likely to adopt them as to get the local tribes to accept Christianity. The white missionaries who sometimes accompanied them to Liberia suffered so from local diseases that they frequently accomplished nothing even if they survived.

Other abolitionists besides Garrison objected to the activities of the colonization society without necessarily faulting its idea of relocation. Benjamin Lundy, one of the earliest outspoken opponents of slavery, tried to find a new home for free blacks close at hand. Hoping to find a good place for relocation, he visited the Mexican territory that eventually became Texas, he went to Canada, and he took a trip to Haiti. Haiti in particular appealed to him. As a Negro nation, free since 1804, it would be a less drastic change than Africa for most American Negroes. After Lundy arranged for blacks to move to Haiti at no expense to themselves, only a few took advantage of the opportunity.

In Liberia the blacks who had been forcibly relocated did enjoy freedom. They might have fared worse. As early as 1817, a shipload of black prisoners from a New York prison were taken to New Orleans to be resold into slavery. Although the harbor authorities there refused them because the ship's captain lacked the proper papers, the captain found a Gulf Coast port where he could transact his business. The smuggling of slaves went on for years, until the end of the Civil War. In New Jersey a kidnapping ring captured free blacks and shipped them at night from Perth Amboy. Conditions on some of the ships proved as horrible as on the slave ships from the Old World, and the

54

voyage down the North American coast, around Florida, and to a receptive port of the Gulf Coast covered more miles than the route from Africa to South Carolina.

The fact that the captain lacked proper papers for the blacks from a New York prison indicates the existence of a "legal" trade in Negroes. Although the United States Government outlawed the African slave trade in 1808, it permitted the shipping of blacks already in bondage from one state to another. In the tobacco-growing states, such as Virginia, Maryland, and North Carolina, the natural increase in blacks provided more than the number of slaves needed. But the birthrate among Negroes in the cotton-producing states farther south did not keep up with the demand for more servants. As a result, Gulf ports received regular shipments of blacks from farther north, and sometimes groups of slaves were herded overland like cattle. Too few people cared that these slaves, many of them separated from their parents, children, or mates, objected to moving. It took the Emancipation Proclamation and the Civil War to end the heartless shifting of slave populations.

Garrison had not exaggerated when he said that blacks objected to removal to Liberia. Within a month after the American Colonization Society was founded, a few thousand free Negroes held a meeting in Philadelphia and discussed the plan. They concluded that it would deprive them of the rights they had earned in the New World and for this reason should be opposed. They drew up a resolution that stated, in part, "without arts, without science, without a proper knowledge of government, to cast into the savage wilds of Africa the free people of color, seems to us the circuitous route through which they must return to perpetual bondage."

A later convention of free blacks in Hartford, Connecticut, opposed the society and its plan with the declaration: "This is our country. . . . Here let us live, and here let us die."

6

RESERVATIONS
Indian Problems

After the American Revolution but before an electoral system selected George Washington as president in 1789, the United States Congress tried to cope with what white people considered the "Indian problem." Officials wanted to keep an eye on the Indians and establish boundaries between the lands of Indians and settlers and also between Indian nations hostile to one another. The idea of reserved areas received consideration, for the first congressmen seldom recognized the Indians' need or desire to roam freely or their right to lands from which they had already been crowded. Nor did Congress foresee the rapidity with which the United States would expand or the restlessness and greed of settlers.

Congress launched the Indian reservation system in 1786 and thought it had settled the "problem." It chose agents, or commissioners, to draw up agreements with the Indians, and these treaties established the early reservations, or agencies as they have also been called. In some instances Congress itself set aside an area to be a reservation, and presidents could also designate reservation locations by decree. All reservations eventually involved treaties, which continued to be written for nearly a century, but white settlers seldom honored them as stringently as they expected the Indians to do.

Among the earliest Indians to have contact with white men north of Florida were the Delaware. By the time of the reservation act, they had been pushed out of Delaware, New Jersey, and eastern Pennsylvania in spite of promises from settlers to leave the lands of the Indians alone. Instead of signing treaties to remain fenced in on lands offered by United States officials, the Delaware kept falling back as settlers pushed west. Even friendly and considerate whites, such as the Quakers, failed to help them find properties that suited them. Wherever they went, they found other tribes already established. Sometimes they received reluctant welcomes and lived at peace for a few years, while at other times they barely had a chance to pause in their wanderings before local Indians attacked them. By the 1800's the wanderers had reached what would become Indiana. Some of the Delaware groups had been displaced for more than a century.

During the first decade of the 1800's, agents appeared among many of the tribes east of the Mississippi to tell them of the extensive and beautiful lands in the territory acquired through the Louisiana Purchase. Among the first who consented to go there were groups of Cherokee, in 1808, and some Choctaw about a year later. The Cherokee and Choctaw, along with the Creek, Chickasaw, and Seminole, made up the Five Civilized Tribes of the Southeast. They had felt pressures from white settlers for decades, and the Seminole were really Creek and other Indians who had fled to the Spanish-held Florida region in the 1760's to live as freely as they had done before whites invaded their original homeland. The Cherokee and Choctaw who agreed to move to the new lands west of the Mississippi did so because of the continuing pressures north of Florida. Before the eastern Indians could be placed in the newly purchased region, however, treaties had to be drawn up with tribes already living there. This took about a decade, with the War of 1812 interfering to slow down negotiations. But that war also made the whites more determined than ever to move the Indians, for numbers of the tribes sided with the British against the Americans.

Although many Cherokee went to Arkansas and some Choctaw and Delaware Indians also moved west before 1820, no large migration occurred. Those who moved found conditions much different from what they expected. The plains lacked the forests in which some tribes had always hunted, and the semiarid soils of the Southwest required irrigation to make agriculture productive. The early arrivals in the Louisiana Purchase territory found survival difficult, news of which discouraged the Indians remaining behind from moving. Even more important, Indians believed the spirits of their ancestors looked after them in the regions where their forefathers had been buried, so they felt strongly about remaining on grounds they had long occupied. Those who had shown a willingness to go had mostly been bands already pushed out of their ancestral territories. Since many whites thought the Indians should convert to Christianity, they frequently remained indifferent to the feelings of the Indians and their respect for the spirits of the dead. They insisted that more Indians should go west and demanded that Congress do something.

In dealing with the Indians who did move, officials showed considerable lack of tact and intelligence. Instead of helping the Delaware to find and acquire lands suitable to their needs, they allowed those eastern Indians to start again their wanderings in search of a homeland. Perhaps the authorities hoped the Sioux and the belligerent tribes of the plains would kill the Delaware or absorb them, thus eliminating them as a problem. Farther south, the Cherokee had to give up their lands in Arkansas. The invention and improvement of the steamboat in the early 1800's made the Mississippi River more and more important for commerce. Eventually some whites thought it unwise to allow Indians who occasionally showed signs of hostility to live near that vital waterway. In addition, authorities and businessmen wanted to establish trading posts and settlements along the banks, so the Cherokee found themselves being moved still farther west. Getting additional eastern tribes to move became increasingly difficult.

In the 1820's the leading Cherokee and Creek chiefs decided they would sell no more land to the whites. Toward the end of 1824 commissioners Duncan Campbell and James Meriwether called the Creek in Georgia to a meeting, hoping to trade land west of the Mississippi to them. The Creek refused. Two months later the commissioners called for another meeting, inviting chiefs sympathetic to the whites as well as minor leaders and men of no rank who were flattered to be included in the discussions. After promising to protect these Indians in case of trouble, the officials talked them into signing a treaty.

The commissioners failed to protect the chiefs who signed, and three of them were killed by the Creek. White settlers then feared an Indian uprising and called for local and federal soldiers to protect them, and the fuss brought into the open how the treaty had been obtained. New meetings took place, during which new treaties were introduced. By playing on suspicions between the Creek and the Cherokee, the agents finally gained ownership of all Creek lands in Georgia. One group of about eight hundred Creek men, women, and children, with black slaves they owned, embarked on steamboats in 1828 and took up new lands in the Oklahoma Territory, often called Indian Territory. Other groups of Creek, Choctaw, and Chickasaw followed during the next few years.

Andrew Jackson won the presidential election of 1828 and took office in 1829. He had gained military honors fighting the Creek during the War of 1812 and the Seminole a few years later and could be counted on to offer little respect for Indian wishes. He openly declared that he would drive the Indians across the Mississippi. In 1830,

Congress passed the Indian Removal Act, taking from the Indians their chance to make a choice. The president received the power to choose the sites to which tribes would go and to request the money for getting them moved. Perhaps the Seneca and the Shawnee remembered the sorry condition of the Delaware who had passed through Ohio decades earlier—a nation without land to call their own. In any case, in 1831 the Shawnee and the Seneca were among the first to agree to move west under the new legislation. Treaties called for tribes to acquire roughly the same amount of territory they occupied at the time they consented to go, but some agents ignored these terms.

The Creek who lived in Alabama refused to be intimidated by the removal law. But Alabama officials established counties and thereafter said that each Indian family had to answer to the laws of the county in which the members lived rather than to tribal chiefs. County courts supported the claims of settlers who moved onto Indian lands, saying the Removal Act made occupancy by Indians illegal. In 1832 some of the chiefs gave up demanding their rights and signed the Removal Treaty. After that, white settlers took over the Indian lands even more aggressively, not waiting for the Creek to move. When Indians resisted, their homes were burned. Without land to farm, they faced starvation and kept alive by stealing. This led to a brief war in which the Creek fought each other as well as the whites and ended as losers. The men, in chains, accompanied by their wives and children had to board ships and go to the Oklahoma Territory. Seeing the hopelessness of trying to remain on their ancestral grounds, other Creek gave in and moved west.

The Cherokee remained on their lands, mainly in Georgia, longer than the Creek. They sometimes helped the white settlers to displace other Indians, perhaps hoping that this would ensure their chances of being allowed to stay. When gold was discovered on part of their lands, their chances of remaining disappeared rapidly. Hoping to complete the removal before the end of 1838, the State of Georgia required all Indians to turn in their arms. Then a force of seven thousand soldiers marched across the state, rounding up the Cherokee and driving them out. General Winfield Scott headed the troops and was considered such a hero for his part in this tragic episode and in various battles with other Indians that he was twice considered as a possible candidate for the United States presidency. The removal proved heartless and brutal. If Indians had failed to make preparations for leaving, the soldiers drove them from their homes without any belongings. Settlers took possession of all goods left behind as well as of the cabins and the land.

The army supplied wagons in which some Indians moved belongings, while others carried possessions in their arms and on their backs. A woman giving birth dropped out of the line of march and had her baby in the bushes, hoping she could later catch up with the slowly moving column. A dying person fell by the side of the trail, and a family member left a bowl of water within reach and then went on. One group crossed a swamp so large that it kept them wading in mucky water for nearly a week. An elderly or particularly weak person might slip beneath the surface and no effort was made at a rescue. Indians and whites along the way stole from the Cherokee, and some of the marchers lost to swindlers what money they carried. About 15,000 Cherokee were driven or transported out of Georgia and neighboring regions, but about a third of them died on the way to Oklahoma. A steamboat on the Mississippi crossing sank and caused at least three hundred to drown. From 1838 on, members of the tribe and their descendants referred to this removal as the Trail of Tears. With the Creek and Cherokee mostly gone and many of the Choctaw moved or moving, the Chickasaw allowed themselves to be removed during 1838. Of the Five Civilized Tribes this left only the Seminole. Spain had ceded Florida to the United States, effective in 1821, so the Seminole now lived in American territory. They resisted giving up their lands, basing their right to them on a treaty of 1834, but the Seminole War of 1835 to 1842 left them powerless. The soldiers drove them onto ships and they went west against their will.

At first the Indians arriving in the Oklahoma Territory had a chance to select settlement sites, but in time, especially during the decade before the Civil War, more and more whites crossed the Mississippi in search of new lands to occupy. As a result, new conflicts with the Indians arose. The United States Government tried to settle these, especially after 1855, by designating specific reservation boundaries and moving the Indians onto these agencies. Once again the Indians discovered that large acreages to which they had been entitled now went to white settlers. For much of the nineteenth century the Indians were kept on their reservations by force or threats of force. Living in closer quarters than previously, they became victims of tuberculosis, whooping cough, measles, and diphtheria. Large reservations usually had a doctor, but he could hardly tend to the needs of thousands of Indians. As many as three fourths of a group might be destroyed at one time.

A white official took charge of each of the early reservations. Often his appointment was a reward for having supported the current president, and was not based on his understanding of Indians, their needs, or their ways of life. In addition to a doctor, the official's few helpers included clerks, an instructor in agricultural methods, a blacksmith, and perhaps a teacher or two. Indians who spoke English usually received paid positions as the official's helpers and translators, as a result of which they often could select the best locations for their houses and the choicest lots for planting gardens. The official appointed Indian judges, but he stood as the final interpreter of the laws and frequently acted as the jury. He could be extremely helpful to the tribes under his jurisdiction or their worst enemy, depending on his inclination. Much of the time, the Indians had

62

enemies worse than the official in charge. Agents could authorize white men to open stores on reservations, and these businessmen often underpaid the Indians for their produce and overcharged them for any goods they bought, keeping them constantly in debt.

The agents in charge of reservations had orders from the military to make the Indians live and dress like white people. Theoretically this would help them adapt more quickly to "civilized" ways and become less rebellious. Some groups proved troublesome, occasionally killing an official or his helpers, but forcing the Indians to dress like whites and live in houses or log cabins hardly made them less belligerent. The new-style homes actually proved a serious mistake. When the Indians had lived in tents and loosely constructed huts they had seldom been bothered by tuberculosis. In the tight frame houses and cabins, where large families lived in close quarters, tuberculosis made its appearance and spread easily. When doctors finally realized what caused the trouble, they won permission for the Indians to return to living in huts and tents. Some Indians grew angry at an order for them to cut off their braids and wear their hair short. Indian men took pride in their long, braided hair and resented having to make a change that was required only as a sign of their giving up their supposedly warlike ways. Farming became another matter for irritation. Tending the fields had been women's work among most tribes, but agricultural instructors said the men had to till the land, plant seeds, keep down weeds, and harvest the crops.

Despite the removal, some Indians always remained in the East. The Cherokee now have reservations in North Carolina, some Seminole live permanently in Florida, and Choctaw occupy agencies in Mississippi. In the North, Ojibway (Chippewa) live on reservations in Wisconsin and Minnesota, and part of the Iroquois nation retains title to lands in New York. Various other agencies have been created east of the Mississippi, but by far the most Indians found themselves west of that boundary by the end of the 1860's. Some areas contained only a few square miles and held two hundred to three hundred people, while other reservations enclosed hundreds of square miles and provided living space for perhaps twenty thousand.

At first, Indians native to the West remained on their lands. But the California gold rush, furs to be trapped in the Rockies, the lure of the Oregon Territory, and plains that could be farmed more easily than forested lands brought the same problems that had been faced earlier in the East. When the Navaho of northeastern Arizona proved warlike, Kit Carson helped to subdue them in 1863. Knowing these Indians well, he did not march to meet them in pitched battle. Instead, he suddenly raided their lands, destroying their crops and herds of sheep and capturing their horses. He relied heavily on bottling up bands of the Navaho in the Canyon de Chelly until they surrendered. In time he held about 8,000 prisoners and forced them to walk to Fort Sumner in New Mexico. This Long Walk caused the Navaho mental as well as physical suffering. They had become famous as horsemen, being among North America's best riders. It humiliated them to have to walk even a few miles, let alone a few hundred. When permitted to return to the Canyon de Chelly Reservation four years later, the Navaho settled down in peace, herding and tending orchards.

All this while the Delaware had continued to wander. They reached as far west as Texas, but there received such unfriendly treatment from local tribes that they agreed to accept a reservation in Kansas. Once on it, they found conditions unsuitable. Late in the 1860's they settled among the Cherokee and other groups in Oklahoma and gradually lost much of their individual identity.

Once they had been given agency areas on which to live, some Indians refused to remain on them. The southern Cheyenne had a large territory in Oklahoma, north of the Cimarron River and south of Kansas. Angered because of white encroachments, because of railroads being planned or built across Indian lands, and because of murderous attacks by volunteer soldiers against northern Cheyenne in Colorado, young men of the southern Cheyenne left the reservation in 1868 to harass white settlements in Kansas. One of their highly respected older leaders, Moke-Tavato, known to whites as Black Kettle, tried to hold them in check but failed. When ordered to report to Fort Cobb, Oklahoma, to account for their actions, the rebellious Cheyenne withdrew south of the Cimarron and established winter camps along the Washita River, where they were joined by groups of Comanche, Arapaho, and Kiowa. Black Kettle reportedly counseled them to make peace with the army, but they refused and he remained with the rebels as leader of one camp.

Career soldier George Custer came to deal with them. Doubtless he arrived in a determined frame of mind. During Indian raids in Kansas in 1867, other officers accused Custer of being ineffective, and after a court-martial he was suspended from service for a year. His supporters claimed that the blame rested on officers of higher rank and Custer served as the whipping boy. He undoubtedly returned to service in 1868 with a fierce desire to prove his abilities and to punish the Indians for his disgrace. He arrived at the Washita River late in November, an impossible time, according to the Indians, to wage war. They assumed that the army intended merely to keep an eye on them. With food scarce for both men and horses at that time of year, they took it for granted that they would have until spring to prepare for battle.

Custer surprised Black Kettle with a dawn attack on November 27. The soldiers killed the chief and others of his group and took numbers of prisoners. The Indians who escaped fled to other camps, and all braves along the Washita began to assemble for an attack against Custer. But the Indians hardly rushed to retaliate, apparently being disheartened by the fact that the whites could fight effectively in winter. Custer, after treating his wounded during the day, drew up his forces as if for another attack that evening. He started an advance toward the nearest Indian camp, while the Indians, amazed at his boldness, prepared to stand their ground. Darkness fell before Custer approached near enough for a skirmish, and the Indians relaxed, assuming the battle would come at dawn. Actually, Custer had no intention of attacking their superior numbers with his tired troops. He intended only to confuse and worry the Indians. As soon as darkness concealed his movements, he turned his soldiers and prisoners aside and marched through the night until, at about two o'clock on the following morning, he allowed the weary army and captives to make camp, miles from the Washita. At the first light of dawn, the warriors along the river took up their stations to defend their camps. Tensely they waited, watching every shadow, every bush blown by the wind. The lighter the sky grew, the more nervous they became. Finally scouts went to investigate and from the tracks discovered what had happened. Being tricked or outwitted often demoralized Indians. This, and Black Kettle's death, and the ease with which Custer had made an attack at that time of year disheartened some to the point of giving up and returning to their reservations. Seeing their numbers decrease, chiefs who had counseled war recognized the futility of further resistance.

A gold rush to the Black Hills of the Dakota Territory caused the Sioux and northern Cheyenne to resist the whites who overran their lands. In 1876, General Custer took part in a campaign to subdue them and made his famous "last stand." After he and his 264 men were wiped out, other officers blamed him for the disaster, but time has shown that in part he was again being made the scapegoat for blunders of other military leaders. Perhaps his death gave a bit of symbolic satisfaction to the Indians, but it hardly made up for the cruelty of the removal program which benefited only selfish, frightened, or greedy whites.

When the time came for Oklahoma to join the Union, the Indians wanted it to be divided into two states, one of them to be an Indian state on an equal basis with all other states. This, at least, might have provided them with some small feeling of having gained something by moving, willingly or otherwise, to the Indian Territory. But they lost even that, and all of Oklahoma joined the Union in 1907 as one state.

Although he did not survive to see the reservation movement developed to the extremes that followed the War of 1812, the Shawnee leader, Tecumseh, said: "These lands are ours. No one has a right to remove us, because we were the first owners. The Great Spirit above has appointed this place for us, on which to light our fires, and here we will remain. As to boundaries, the Great Spirit above knows no boundaries, nor will his red people acknowledge any."

Following the War of 1812, Pushmataha, of the Choctaw, finally saw the necessity of objecting to the demands of the Americans. He never became a fiery speaker like Tecumseh, but in his quiet way he expressed the Indian point of view when opposing the United States president, whom the Indians had been taught to call "the great father." "This day we have made up our minds . . . to answer our great father's talk. Children, even after they have grown to be men, ought to regard the advice of their father. . . . I am sorry I cannot comply with the request of my father. . . . We wish to remain here . . . and do not wish to be transplanted to another soil."

7

DEPART OR DIE
The Mormons

The desire for freedom of religion had much to do with the founding of the United States. Yet religious persecution also played a part. It wasn't until 1821 that New York State legislated to end discrimination against Roman Catholics. Just a year before that, in upper New York, a fifteen-year-old farmhand—Joseph Smith—prayed to God for guidance in choosing the right church and received the answer, he reported, to join no church at all. Three years later an angel, Moroni, supposedly told him where he would find golden plates on which were inscribed *The Book of Mormon,* which Smith published in 1830. He founded his church of Latter-day Saints on April 6 of that year. His followers called themselves Saints, while outsiders referred to them as Mormons when not calling them murderers, thieves, and other derogatory terms.

New Yorkers grew to dislike their Mormon neighbors and caused them to depart, after which they settled in Ohio. Here, too, they found unfriendly surroundings, but Smith cheered his followers with reports of visions he had received concerning Missouri. There they would find Zion, or God's Kingdom, and as early as 1831 some of them went in search of it. Smith, reportedly in a vision, saw the site of Independence, Missouri, as the location of the original Garden of Eden, while Adam's burial place was farther north, in the vicinity of Gallatin. An unincorporated territory, northwestern Missouri provided large acreages available at reasonable prices, but it lay within the United States. The newcomers sometimes behaved as though it didn't and soon found themselves in conflict with their neighbors. Mormons called the Missourians Gentiles—a term they used for all non-Mormons—although after trouble began they sometimes referred to them as "pukes."

Many factors created the problems in Missouri. Just when Mormon men started taking more than one wife is unclear, but some of them did it secretly and others not so secretly before they reached Missouri. Their neighbors began to suspect the men of trying to seduce any pretty girls they met without intentions of marrying. Joseph Smith originally objected to the practice of polygamy, but later he said a vision had told him the Saints could marry more than one woman. Critics said he conveniently had the vision after becoming infatuated with a teen-age girl when he already had one wife, Emma. Since United States law said a man could have only one mate, the Missourians could openly object to polygamy. Other areas for complaint revealed fears and prejudices. Related to plural marriages were the large numbers of children in many Mormon families. Men with several wives sometimes fathered dozens of children, and Missourians feared the state would soon have a Latter-day Saint population larger than its non-Mormon group.

The growing numbers of Mormons would want more land, which they were already buying up or trading for at a remarkable rate. In addition, the numbers of Mormons arriving from the East after the first newcomers received permission to settle took the Missourians by surprise. The Gentiles had failed to anticipate the size of the group, which attracted converts rapidly after its early years. The old settlers worried that they would be crowded out by the recent arrivals. According to Missourian reports, the newcomers often managed to set their fences, when enclosing their purchases, around a few more acres than they had really acquired. This may have been true on occasion, for the Saints considered the land holy to their faith and thought the local people should give it up more willingly than they proved ready to do. Disputes over where fences belonged led to fistfights at first but soon brought on skirmishes with clubs, knives, or guns. As soon as they settled down, Mormons started seeking converts. It seemed to Missourians that they worked most diligently on families who owned choice properties. This apparent effort to win land as well as followers gave one more indication of Mormon efforts to crowd out the original settlers.

The Mormons admittedly wanted a country of their own. They wanted to elect all its officials, write all its laws, and answer to no other authority than their own. As soon as they could participate in local elections, they entered their own candidates and turned out in full force on election day to vote for them. Quite rapidly, the Mormons won important positions in local governments. In time they controlled a region just south of Gallatin, which they reportedly wanted to call Mormon County in 1838, although it is known as Caldwell County today. With one small area in their hands, they formed a militia of their own and based it in that county. The few Gentile families within the region's boundaries lived in fear of their safety. On election day in Gallatin, Missourians decided they would stop the political advances of the Latter-day Saints. Massing around the polling place, they prepared to keep the Mormons away. When the first Mormon approached, they informed him that Mormons and "niggers" weren't allowed to vote. The man tried to reach the poll anyway, but the Gentiles knocked him down. As he fell, he called for help, and about three dozen club-wielding Saints rushed to his aid. After they drove off the Missourians, they all proceeded to vote.

Missouri had entered the Union as a slave state in 1821.

70

The Mormons sometimes helped blacks obtain their freedom and gave no assistance to Missourians searching for runaways. The Missourians, who claimed that Mormon men frequently treated their wives like slaves, thought the Mormons helped blacks escape in order to weaken the economy of individuals, counties, and the state. This may have had a basis of truth. In addition, the Mormons dealt kindly with the Indians, who were being crowded out of their lands by the Missourians. Quite probably the Mormons encouraged the Indians to fight back. This too may have been done to weaken the local economy, for it seldom benefited the Indians.

When the first Mormons arrived, the Missourians saw them as new sources for business opportunities. Soon they discovered that the Mormons needed almost nothing from outsiders. Instead of hiring local labor, the newcomers relied entirely on one another. It startled and angered Missourians to see Mormon women pulling plows. In good seasons, the hardworking Mormons had larger crops than their neighbors. In poor seasons, the Saints struggled almost day and night to salvage something and never seemed to have the small yields of the Gentiles. Instead of buying foods or goods from Missourians, the Mormons traded among themselves or did without. Almost as soon as they built houses, they also erected mills, smithies, and harness shops. But when they had anything for sale, the Mormons dealt with the Missourians and proved to be shrewd. Rarely could a Missourian feel he got the better end of a deal. In time, if a Mormon flour mill seemed to be taking business away from one run by a Missourian, the Mormon mill might go up in flames. When the Mormons gathered to erect a replacement, one of their barns, corncribs, or houses might catch fire while they were busy at the millsite. They were not a people to turn the other cheek. A Missourian could expect to discover his mill, barn, or house in flames within a night or two.

The Mormons organized vigilante groups for retalia-

71

tion, but these groups carried out secret missions when there were no acts for which to retaliate. In time the name for the Mormon raiders became the Sons of Dan, or Danites, after a prophet in *The Book of Mormon* named Daniel. Their main base became Caldwell County, although every community had vigilante members. Torture became a practice among the Danites. On occasion, apprehending a Missourian by himself, they scarred his face or body, or perhaps they rendered him incapable of fathering children. Missourians tarred and feathered Mormon men and raped the women. After they learned that Mormon women and children could be as belligerent as the men, the Missourians beat and whipped them.

Joseph Smith located at a settlement called Far West. This was to serve as temporary headquarters until he could gain permission to build a temple farther south on the site of what he claimed had been the Garden of Eden. After Missourians began to plan and organize regular attacks against the Mormons, numbers of refugees arrived in the vicinity of Far West. Smith, who apparently had never discouraged the Danites, now openly encouraged them, saying the Missourians had declared war. War it proved to be. It started in 1837, when the Missourians turned from trying to hold the Mormons in check to actually driving them out of the state. In that year the country slipped into a major depression, and it infuriated Missourians to see the Mormons generally thriving when most other people suffered from lack of trade. The war reached its peak in 1838.

At a village called Shoal Creek, or Haun's Mills, only a few Mormons lived, but they ground flour, sawed lumber, and shod horses for farmers in a large area round about. During 1837 and 1838, Missourians looked on this small center as a growing threat to Gentile existence. Finally a mob went to destroy it. Mormon women and children hid in the woods while the men barricaded themselves in the blacksmith shop. After the Mormons exhausted their ammunition and ceased to return fire, the Missourians

72

stormed the smithy and found only one obvious survivor, a ten-year-old boy who had hidden under the bellows. The invaders reportedly shot him and left. As soon as they dared, the people hiding in the woods returned to the village and discovered that most of their friends and relatives were dead. Between one and two dozen men, according to conflicting reports, had pretended to be dead after being wounded. The women gave what medical attention they could, but more men died during the next few days.

At Whitmer, where Kansas City now stands, Missourians attacked quietly at night. When they started to tear down houses and beat any Mormons they could catch, shooting broke out. There were dead and wounded on both sides, but the Missourians may have suffered the most. Those who escaped without serious injuries resolved to return the next night and make a better showing. They gathered new helpers and waited for darkness to shield their approach. Apparently a shower of meteorites fell into the earth's atmosphere just when the attackers reached Whitmer. As friction against the atmosphere turned the pieces of stone to white-hot streaks across the sky, the Missourians took the fiery display as a warning and slipped away, leaving the Mormons in peace that night.

Although some state officials objected to the treatment of the Mormons, many approved. Governor Lilburn W. Boggs expressed the hatred within the state when he ordered out the militia, stating, "The Mormons must be treated as enemies, and must be exterminated or driven from the state." The day had passed, if it ever existed, when Mormons had a choice between changing religion or leaving. The choice had become between leaving the state or dying. With their determination to build a temple at Joseph Smith's Garden of Eden site, the Mormons intended to keep their religion, their lands, and their lives. Smith called on all Saints with guns to join the militia in Caldwell County. With Colonel George Hinkle in charge, these troops prepared to resist the attack of the Missouri militia led by General Samuel Lucas. Hinkle met with Lucas, after which he reported to Smith that the Missourian wanted to try settling the trouble peacefully. Smith and four other Mormon leaders went to confer with the general. According to one story, Hinkle turned the Mormon leaders over to Lucas as prisoners, supposedly to save his own hide. In another report, Smith and his assistants negotiated with Lucas and finally agreed to surrender themselves for trial as thieves, rapists, and murderers if the rest of the Mormons would be allowed to leave the state alive.

With Smith locked up, Brigham Young began to show the qualities of leadership on which the Mormons later relied. It is thought that he played a major part in directing the departure from Missouri. Rather than go west into unknown territory, the Mormons backtracked to Illinois, where they camped for a matter of weeks at Quincy. They made the trip in the dead of winter, mainly between December 1838 and March 1839, with Missourians sometimes harassing them as they went. Even in good weather it would have been a difficult trip under the circumstances, but in freezing temperatures with drifts of snow the Mormons suffered constant weariness, hunger, and sickness. When they reached the Mississippi River, they could sometimes walk across to Quincy on the ice.

Most of the Mormons had to leave Missouri without many possessions. In some places, the Missourians forced them at gunpoint to sign over deeds to their farms. In other places, the local people occupied the land without obtaining title to it. This, Missourians said, paid for the damage the Mormons had done in their years in the state. All the Mormons received orders to turn in guns and knives before starting the trek, for the Missourians feared that the refugees would attack settlements along the way or possibly try to rescue Smith. Although some hid weapons and managed to get them to Illinois, large numbers had to use sticks as hunting implements. In the deep snow, they might be lucky enough to club a rabbit or a squirrel, but some of the time they must have been helped by kindly Missourians who recognized the severity of their ordeal. After arriving in Illinois, they received help from some people of Quincy until they could make a new start.

In villages where Mormons hesitated, Missourians usually burned one house with all furniture and goods in it as a warning of what would happen to all houses unless the people left. This generally started the Saints on their way. Some shooting occurred, but it cost the Mormons lives and the weapons they needed for hunting, so they learned to suppress their anger. Even as the people left their homes, the Missourians started tearing the buildings down, carting away all furniture, lumber, and stones they could use. Cattle, horses, and other livestock, along with hay, corn, and other stored grains and foodstuffs, immediately became the prizes of the Missourians. Wherever the state militia marched in search of Saints to rout out, it destroyed much in the way of foods and property, preventing local people and Mormons alike from benefiting from it. The soldiers forced their attentions on the women, especially the girls. At Far West, it was later reported, the troops lashed seven teen-age girls to benches in the schoolhouse and took turns raping them through the course of one night.

As spring came, the Mormons moved north from Quincy. Above Keokuk, Iowa, the Mississippi formed a sweeping arc around a marshy neck of Illinois land, back of which rose a hill. A few Gentile families had made a settlement here, which they called Commerce, in order to carry on trade with boats passing on the river. The Mormons saw beauty in the spot, as well as commercial possibilities, and decided they had found the new site in which to settle. The people of Commerce either withdrew and left the peninsula to the Mormons or became absorbed into the city that promptly started to grow. When

75

the spring weather warmed the boggy land, mosquitoes of the area provided the Mormons with a bloodthirsty welcome. Many of the people had already fallen sick, probably with typhoid and hepatitis from drinking or washing foods in polluted water of the swampy lowland. Now the mosquitoes presented them with malaria. The Mormons, and most other people, had a poor understanding of their ailments, thinking them caused by miasma, which is what they called the vapor that hovered over swampy places. But they struggled to stay on their feet and work at least a few hours a day. At first they camped in tents and lean-tos while they started log cabins and wooden-frame houses. Stores, schools, and more important buildings required stone, which they gathered from the surrounding territory, trespassing on Illinois farms to find what they wanted. Almost from the beginning they acquired the enmity of their new neighbors.

To prepare the land for farming, the Mormons drained the marshes, a wise action for the sake of their health. They left the mosquitoes with few places to survive, and the insects died out or found other locations to fit their needs. When Joseph Smith came to join them in a few weeks after escaping, or being allowed to escape, from prison, the area had been changed from a marsh to an attractive community with green fields stretching away from the river and up the hill. Impressed, Smith called the town Nauvoo, which, he said, was a Hebrew word for "beautiful." In time it became the largest city of Illinois, accommodating more than twenty thousand people and boasting clean, well-constructed houses of brick and stone. Atop the hill rose an attractive temple. Vineyards and orchards were added to the croplands and gardens.

Before he had been in Illinois long, Smith called the Mormons together and warned them against crowding their neighbors. Again some of the Saints tried to fence in more acres than they purchased, and they carried off not only stones but lumber and perhaps a calf they found on a Gentile's property. Smith said they had been right in doing such things across the river, for the Missourians had waged war against them, but the people of Illinois had shown better manners. However, some of his followers continued to give the whole group a bad name.

Feeling that Missouri owed them large sums for their lost properties, the Saints stole goods from riverboats destined for St. Louis and other Missouri ports. From time to time, bands of Missourians slipped across the river, came close to Nauvoo under the cover of nearby forests and brushlands, and captured Mormons who might be out hunting alone or in small groups. They then demanded goods in return for those stolen. Sometimes they found stolen property hidden in the woods, but they seldom stopped at retrieving the shipment. They generally gave the Mormons some punishment, often using torture. Since the Missourians felt the people of Illinois should be more active in curtailing the thefts of Missouri-bound shipments, ill feelings developed between the two states. This prompted the Illinoisans to blame the Mormons and to treat them less kindly.

Smith and a few leaders went to Washington, D.C., in the hope that Congress would force Missouri to pay for its heartless treatment of the Saints. The Mormons drew up reports of what had happened, as they saw it, and presented these as the basis of their claims. Much of what they reported showed an overbearing concern about property and economic considerations. Several congressmen decided a Mormon man would prefer to have his wife or daughter raped than to have his possessions damaged. It also became public knowledge that the Danites had launched acts of violence for their own gains rather than in retaliation for acts committed against the Mormons. These and other disclosures cast doubt over the religion as well as over everyone concerned with it as far as Congress could see and defeated Joseph Smith's case. He also lost any chance of support for the right to return to Missouri

77

to build a temple on the Garden of Eden site.

In May 1843 a would-be assassin attempted to kill Lilburn Boggs, though he was no longer governor of Missouri. Missourians felt certain that Smith had ordered the shooting and wanted the governor of Illinois to turn him over to them. Tensions along the Mississippi mounted. At about the same time various Saints began to have doubts about Smith and about the Mormon religion. They published a newspaper in Nauvoo expressing their views, and the city officials immediately had the press demolished and its building burned. The governor of Illinois then warned the Saints that attacks on freedom of the press could not be tolerated. If necessary, he would call out the militia to protect the publishers, which, he said, might lead to the destruction of Nauvoo and the extermination of its residents. Joseph Smith saw this as a repetition of what had happened in Missouri, but this time he did not stay to fight.

Smith started west to seek a new "paradise" in Mexican-held lands, where he hoped to establish Zion outside the control of the United States. On his first night, a messenger from his wife, Emma, caught up with him in Iowa and warned him that the people of Illinois, learning of his departure, were preparing to attack Nauvoo. Smith returned to the city, and he and three other leaders were taken to Carthage, Illinois. Here a mob rushed the jail and shot them. Another mob marched on Nauvoo and caused considerable damage in one section of it. Knowing the futility of a house-to-house stand after their Missouri experience, the Saints packed what belongings they could into wagons and left. Nauvoo became the nation's most beautiful ghost town.

Smith had wanted a son who bore his name to succeed him, but this boy was only twelve years old in June 1844 when his father was killed. Emma and her children remained in Illinois after most of the Mormons went west under the leadership of Brigham Young. Other members of the faith who also remained behind formed the Reorganized Church of Jesus Christ of Latter-day Saints, and young Joseph Smith became its president in 1860. He filled the office honorably for more than fifty years. Unlike his determined, dictatorial father, he did much to make Mormonism respected throughout the United States.

With travel so easy in the 1970's, it is difficult to imagine what people faced during a forced migration more than a century and a quarter ago. Thomas Kane, a military officer, came upon a party of Saints driven from Nauvoo. Perhaps his comments can be considered more objective than those of either the Mormons themselves or the people of Illinois and Missouri who forced them to move. "Dreadful, indeed, was the suffering of these forsaken beings; bowed and cramped by cold and sunburn, alternating as each weary day and night dragged on, they were, almost all of them, the crippled victims of disease. They were there because they had no homes, nor hospital, nor poor-house, nor friends to offer them any. They could not satisfy the feeble cravings of their sick; they had no bread to quiet the fractious hunger cries of their children. Mothers and babes, daughters and grand-parents, all of them alike, were bivouacked in tatters, wanting even covering to comfort those whom the sick shiver of fever was searching to the marrow."

8

"FREE" BLACKS
Emancipation?

At the age of twenty-one, William King, an Irishman educated in Scotland for the Presbyterian ministry, came to the United States. Two years later, in 1835, he settled in Louisiana as rector of a boys' academy and soon fell in love with the daughter of a slave owner. His sweetheart took it for granted that she would have blacks to look after her, which caused the romance to falter. King found it difficult to believe that one person should own another. But he feared he might lose the girl to another man if he hesitated too long, so he proposed and they were married. His bride brought fifteen blacks with her, and William King unwillingly became a slave owner.

When it became necessary for King to return to Scotland for additional schooling, he hoped to release the Negroes. But Louisiana law would not allow him to free the blacks at that time. He could sell them to other owners, but this he refused to do, fearing that they might end up in the hands of people who would treat them cruelly. Soon the young minister hit on a plan. He could buy a small plantation and put the blacks on it, letting them operate it and live on the profits they made. His father-in-law, who had begun to accept his views about slavery, agreed to watch over the plantation. This revolutionary

80

idea horrified King's neighbors and friends, and they discouraged him. They probably told him that the blacks would ruin the land, burn down the buildings, or do so little work that they would starve. However, he had watched them enough to know them better than many people who had lived around slaves all their lives. King bought land and established the blacks on it.

With that problem taken care of, King started with his wife and son to visit his parents, who now lived in Ohio. On the way, his son "took fever and died." His wife was none too well either, but once they reached Edinburgh she seemed to improve. A daughter was born to them in Scotland, but during their second year there both his wife and daughter died. Despite his tragedies, King continued with his studies and completed them in 1846. He accepted a ministerial post in Canada and went there by way of Louisiana. By this time his father-in-law had also passed away, but on his plantation the blacks proved to be thriving without an overseer. Happy in knowing that they could manage by themselves, King went to Canada and took up his new work.

The following year word came for King to return and help to settle his father-in-law's estate, at which time King's parishioners learned that he owned slaves. Most of them were surprised, and some grew quite angry. Slavery had seldom been viewed kindly in Canada. King informed them that Louisiana would not permit him to free his slaves but the laws had been rewritten enough for him to take them to non-slave territory and release them from bondage. As a result, he intended to bring them back to Canada. This caused even more consternation within his congregation. He agreed to resign his post, but on his return he hoped that they would be understanding and offer it to him again. They gave him no answer. He left for Louisiana without knowing whether or not he would have a job on his return.

In Louisiana some of his slaves objected to moving

north. They had always lived in a warm climate and they had no friends or relatives in Canada. After convincing several of them to go, King decided to take the rest against their will. Back in Ontario, some of his old parishioners grumbled. He saw a long stretch of tensions ahead—for himself, for his former slaves, and for other blacks arriving in Canada by way of the Underground Railroad. He realized the cruelty of turning the blacks loose among strangers, and he decided to devote his life to aiding them.

King helped start a company for assisting blacks, and in 1850 he bought eighteen square miles of land near Elgin on which to settle them. With King as superintendent, the blacks cleared the land and built homes. They called it the Buxton Settlement, after England's Sir Thomas Buxton, who had fought for antislavery legislation. Settlement land sold for $2.50 an acre, and King's fifteen blacks easily bought lots with the money saved when they had operated the plantation in Louisiana. But many runaway blacks arrived without money. King helped them find work in railroad construction, where there always seemed to be a need for laborers. After the Civil War many former slaves returned to the United States to find friends and relatives, but others remained in Canada, as did William King. Amid all the tragic stories of ways in which blacks found themselves shuttled about, King's history is a particularly happy one. The people he moved definitely found themselves better off than they would have been in Louisiana.

When Harriet Beecher Stowe published *Uncle Tom's Cabin* in 1852, she knew nothing of William King's efforts. But her interest in abolition brought his story to her attention before long, and reportedly she used a few elements of it for the basis of another novel, *Dred; a Tale of the Great Dismal Swamp.*

When Edward Clayton, the hero, outlines his plan to help the slaves placed under his care, his closest friend becomes alarmed, as did King's friends.

"You will be a mark for arrows, both sides. You will offend all your neighbors by doing better than they do. You will bring your negroes up to a point in which they will meet the current of the whole community against them, and meanwhile you will get no credit from the Abolitionists. They will call you a cut-throat, pirate, sheep-stealer, and all the rest of their elegant little list of embellishments, all the same. You'll get a state of things that nobody can manage but yourself, and you by the hardest; and then you'll die, and it'll all run to the devil faster than you run it up."

Eventually Edward Clayton's life is in danger, and he is so well known that he can hardly make a move to help the blacks without being stopped. Taking some blacks with him, he leaves for Canada, where he buys land and helps the former slaves to settle.

William King wanted to free blacks or remove them from slaveholding states, but Harriet Beecher Stowe saw the larger issue of getting Southern laws rewritten. Consequently, she gave Edward Clayton a very different life from King's, on which she based it, and the move to Canada ends the novel, although it began a new life for William King. Both in the real-life story and in the fictional one the blacks taken north did benefit.

9

AN
"ODIOUS ORDER"

Jews Rejected

Headquarters Thirteenth Army Corps,
Department of the Tennessee,
Oxford, Miss., Dec. 17, 1862:

General Order No. 11.—The Jews, as a class, violating every regulation of trade established by the Treasury Department, also Department orders, are hereby expelled from the Department within Twenty-four (24) hours from the receipt of this order by Post Commander.

They will see that all this class of people are furnished with passes and required to leave, and any one returning after such notification will be arrested and held in confinement until an opportunity occurs of sending them out as prisoners, unless furnished with permits from these headquarters.

No pass will be given these people to visit headquarters for the purpose of making application for trade permits. By order of

Maj.-Gen. Grant

With this order, reprinted from *The New York Times* of January 18, 1863, Ulysses S. Grant set off a war within a war. No statistics show how many Jews departed, but some did. Jewish families of Paducah, Kentucky, who had lived there for generations packed what belongings they could and left their homes. As an editorial in *The New York*

Times pointed out, "They had nothing whatever to do with Grant or his army." Those near Grant's headquarters in Mississippi also prepared to leave. Fortunately, the order promptly came to the attention of officials in Washington. The *Times* indicated that President Lincoln himself canceled it at once, but some historians now credit other officials, particularly Secretary of War Edwin Stanton, and it may have taken two weeks to get it withdrawn.

Jews throughout the nation angrily voiced their opinions of Grant. And some blamed officials in Washington, thinking that the order would never have been written unless the general felt he had administration backing. This underestimates Grant's ability to be dictatorial, though there may have been some grounds for such an accusation. Besides infuriating the Jews, the order and its cancelation led to disharmony among them. A committee in New York sent the officials in Washington a message of thanks for killing the order. Other Jews attacked the committee, saying they should give "no thanks for an act of simple and imperative justice." At times the dissent among themselves became so strong that they nearly forgot about Grant and what the newspapers termed his "odious order." When they did think of the general, many of them demanded his dismissal.

The writer of the *Times* editorial said that one objection to the order was its "atrocious disregard of the simplest rules of English composition. To be dealt harshly with is bad enough, but to be vilified in execrable English is cruel, if not unusual, punishment." The editor went on to find fault with the logic of the order, in the matter of permits, as expressed at the end of paragraph two and in paragraph three. The writer thought it "mortifying" to know that a department of war was under the jurisdiction of a man who could not produce better English and clearer sense than the order exhibited. The worst thing about it, however, was Grant's condemning of Jews *as a class*. Admittedly, "Gen. Grant may have been harassed by hangers-on of his army, who were swindlers and extortionists. It was desirable that he should be rid of such. But will he say that all the swindlers that beset him are Jews?" The *Times* certainly thought otherwise. "All swindlers are not Jews. All Jews are not swindlers." Grant's order harked back to the twelfth, thirteenth, and fourteenth centuries, when England, France, and Austria banished Jews. No wonder the nation reacted with shock, Gentiles and Jews alike, since "it remained for the freest Government on earth to witness a momentary revival of the spirit of the medieval ages."

The *Times* also decried the effect the general's order could have on foreign governments. The Jews holding high offices in many European nations might influence their countrymen against the Union cause. The Confederacy had been trying to enlist help from some of those countries, and Grant should have thought of this. He also should have considered that "The Rothschilds wield a power in the financial world that is well nigh omnipotent to raise or destroy the credit of any nation." Any order punishing a whole class of people did "gross violence to our free institutions" and was completely unjust, so the editorial writer praised Lincoln for saving the country from a "blot."

Grant's biographers as well as the historians of the Civil War consider the matter in a light missed by newspapers of the day. There were men in both the North and the South who put making money ahead of any thought about ending the killing or settling the secession question. With Union vessels trying to blockade southern coasts, the Confederacy had trouble selling its cotton to raise badly needed money. Southern cotton dealers attempted to get their product into the hands of Northern dealers, who would sell it wherever they could. These dealers undermined Union efforts to bankrupt the Confederacy and bring the war to a rapid finish, and most officers and officials of the Union disliked them. Some were Jews, many were not, but it became a careless practice to refer to all dealers coming down from the North as Jews (Jewish people should have been angered by that in itself). Grant wanted these traders, as a class, eliminated from the war zone.

Possibly Grant didn't write the order. He may have dictated it in a hurry, expecting the writer to put it into proper English and to say "traders" rather than "Jews." In fact, in some modern books there is a version of the order that is in better English than the one in the *Times,* so it is difficult to know exactly what was written, by whom it was written, or exactly what it meant. But in every case it did say "Jews" and gave all Jewish people logical grounds for furious objections.

Grant's was not the first such order during the war. Colonel John Dubois, with headquarters at Holly Springs, Mississippi, had tried shortly before to rid his town of outsiders "having no honest means of support." He had called them "vagrants," "speculators," and "Jews," and it had been Grant who killed Dubois' order. Obviously it referred to traders profiting on the war rather than just to Hebraic peoples and followers of Judaism. Grant might have benefited by paying more attention to the wording of Dubois' order, thereby possibly making his own somewhat clearer and less irritating. At the same time, we are left wondering why Grant revoked that order but soon issued one with a similar purpose. Some historians think that one of his relatives, perhaps his own father, tried to help certain Jews "make use of" the general's high position to obtain trading permits. Humiliated and infuriated by this treachery within his own family, Grant could have scribbled off or hurriedly dictated General Order No. 11.

The *Times* editorial indicated raging anger among Jewish people at the time. Some modern writers think the real furor came later. In 1868, Grant became a nominee for the United States presidency, and he had a wide circle of enemies of all races and religions to dredge up every blunder he ever made. In spite of this, the people of the United States kept him in office for eight years, giving him ample opportunities to make up for old blunders or to create new ones.

Had General Order No. 11 stood, it definitely would have brought unforgivable hardships to thousands of people. It should give us encouragement today to know that unfair forced relocation can sometimes be prevented.

10
IN THE
NAME OF PROGRESS
Canadian Métis

Almost from the first, Europeans reaching North America moved inland, searching for something more than what they had. If it wasn't a Fountain of Youth or gold, it was better soil or streams richer in beaver. At first they went on foot, on horseback, or in canoes. Later they used wagons and, in time, stagecoaches and river steamers. Stagecoach and steamer displaced few people, but the development of railroads drastically changed lives and whole landscapes. A railroad company never curved its tracks around a man's house or farm if it stood in the way of what was considered progress.

North of the 49th parallel and west of the newly confederated country of Canada stretched a great territory called Rupert's Land. England's Charles II had given his relative Prince Rupert a charter for trading rights in the lands of the Hudson Bay basin, and for two centuries Rupert's Hudson's Bay Company ruled this region. French, English, and Scottish fur traders passed through the area, leaving behind many half-breed children. Some foreigners settled with or near the Indians, and by the time Ontario, Quebec, New Brunswick, and Nova Scotia confederated in 1867 to form the Dominion of Canada, Rupert's Land had a scattered but permanent population of whites, half-breeds, and Indians. Because the French half-breeds devoted part of each year to extensive buffalo hunts, some officials of Canada considered them nomadic rather than settled. Yet these métis maintained houses and made some efforts at farming.

Many métis lacked papers to show ownership of their land. They squatted on it and held it only by right of occupation. As Canadians moved west from Ontario and eastern Canada, they encroached upon the métis' lands and at the same time called for a new rule to replace the lax control of the Hudson's Bay Company. When the Canadians petitioned for annexation to Canada, the métis could get more signatures on petitions of their own in opposition to a change of government. Since many of them could neither read nor write more than their names, they relied on leaders who could. One such man, Louis Riel, had received an education in Montreal and quickly became important among the French half-breeds, who felt themselves being forced off their properties. With his command of English, French, and Indian languages, Riel acted as interpreter. But because of a small amount of Indian blood in his veins, he considered himself a métis and at no time remained neutral. While interpreting, he took sides and endeavored to swing negotiations in favor of the French half-breeds.

Between 1867 and 1870, traffic from Canada to Rupert's Land increased. Most travelers found the overland trip too rugged, since they had to make nearly fifty portages and spend two or more months in reaching the village where Winnipeg now stands. They could make the trip more easily and in a week or two by taking a Great Lakes steamer to Duluth, Minnesota, and going north and west from there on a United States railway. Disagreements might close the United States route to Canadian citizens, however, and so the value of a Canadian rail link became apparent.

The idea of a railroad frightened the métis. In the

United States the Union Pacific had been built across the continent in the 1860's. Hired buffalo hunters destroyed herds to keep them from walking or stampeding across rail lines. And farmers put up fences to keep their livestock from being killed by locomotives. Buffalo hunts of the sort on which the métis depended for food and clothing had become impossible in the vicinity of United States rail lines. In addition, some farmers had had to move from their land or at least surrender part of it, and now and then a family had been made to tear down its house and build in another spot. A railroad across Rupert's Land would end buffalo hunts there and force the métis to retreat west or take up an entirely new way of life. Without papers to support their land claims, what chance would they have of holding their properties or of receiving pay for giving them up? A Winnipeg newspaper, the *Nor'Wester*, added to the fears of the half-breeds when it stated bluntly, "The indolent and the careless, like the native tribes of the country, will fall back before the march of a superior intelligence." The newspaper welcomed the prospect of a railroad and wanted the half-breeds to have to relocate.

In 1867 the métis received a taste of what improved transportation facilities might mean. Locusts plagued the countryside, ruining crops and bringing starvation. The Canadian government voted to contribute seeds to help the sufferers, but felt that it should in some way receive payment for its generosity. Officials decided to build a road from Lake of the Woods, on the border between Minnesota and Rupert's Land, to the Red River of the North. The métis and other farmers of the area could do the work to pay for the wheat seeds and food sent them. Some métis had to give up their lands to make way for the road, and the amount of work they did came to more than the value of the wheat they received. To complicate the annoying situation, the half-breeds heard rumors that Indians had sold to outsiders land to which the métis laid claim. Bickering resulted, and when the overseers of the

91

roadway sided with the Indians the métis drove the officials out of the Red River Settlement, as the area around Winnipeg was called. Besides, the half-breeds by this time suspected that the road would allow Canadians to enter and take control of their region.

The Minister of Public Works in Ottawa, failing to appreciate the tense situation, ordered a survey of the area west of Ontario. Through it the government would know exactly what lands it would acquire if Canada took over Rupert's Land. A survey would also benefit railway companies and road builders when it came time to extend transportation routes toward the Pacific. The half-breeds thought that the arrival of survey teams meant a Canadian take-over without waiting for negotiations with the Hudson's Bay Company to be completed. They threatened to use force to stop the work and repeated their wish to be included in negotiations between the Hudson's Bay Company and the Canadian government. The surveying stopped only temporarily, and the métis began to think they needed a government of their own if they expected representation in the negotiations.

Surveyors reached the farm of a cousin of Louis Riel, who came as interpreter, but he really hoped to halt the survey again. The métis stood on the surveying chain and kept the workers from moving forward while Riel informed the workers that attempts to proceed would result in trouble. The métis appeared to have won a victory, and this emboldened them to try for other gains. A lieutenant governor had started west from Canada, to be on hand the moment the Hudson's Bay Company gave up its control. This, the Canadian government hoped, would discourage factions in Rupert's Land from setting up governments of their own. Unfortunately, the man picked, William McDougall, had been in charge of the unfinished road from Lake of the Woods to Winnipeg, and he was known as a supporter of railroads. He had thoroughly angered the métis while overseeing the road construction, so he had

92

neither their trust nor their friendship. They decided to keep him from entering their territory.

For bargaining purposes, the métis hastily formed a government. They chose Riel as secretary, but in practice he held more authority than the president. He ordered a barricade thrown across the completed section of the road and sent word for McDougall to turn back. A strong-willed man who believed he had right on his side, the lieutenant governor ignored this order and marched forward. Expecting to find a few armed men cowering behind a makeshift wall of logs, he felt genuine alarm when he had to face more than a hundred métis boldly massed across the route and aiming rifles from behind nearly every tree on both sides of the road. He turned back in humiliation.

McDougall should have realized that the half-breeds could produce an army. Of about ten thousand people living in Rupert's Land at the end of the 1860's, whites amounted to fewer than two thousand. English and Scottish half-breeds also numbered less than the métis, so Riel had several thousand people from whom to recruit soldiers. About a mile from the village of Winnipeg stood a large fort, Garry, from which even a weak force should be able to exert its influence over Rupert's Land. Riel led part of his force to the fort and brazenly informed the commanding officer that they had come to protect it. The surprised officer let them take over. Riel now hoped that Ottawa would include the métis in any negotiations related to Rupert's Land. At the same time Riel recognized the value of support from all the inhabitants of the territory. However, people of British descent knew that Riel considered himself a métis, in spite of his small amount of Cree blood, and they held back. Riel liked to be treated with respect, even with adulation. It angered him when the non-métis groups proved standoffish, and at times he acted toward them as high-handedly as he accused Ottawa of treating the métis.

McDougall devised a plan to force the métis to acknowledge him as lieutenant governor of Rupert's Land. He would issue a proclamation saying that Queen Victoria had transferred the region to the Canadian government. Rumors indicated that the queen would do just that at any moment. McDougall doubted that Riel would defy the wishes of Britain's queen, so he saw no reason to wait for the actual transfer to occur. Ottawa officials advised McDougall to wait, but the lieutenant governor wanted to assume his duties as well as his title. On the basis of newspaper reports and his private correspondence with friends in Canada and England, he felt positive that the queen would act on December 1, 1869. When he issued his proclamation, Riel and the métis waited for official word to come from Ottawa. It did not arrive, and the French half-breeds suspected McDougall of fraud.

Thinking that time would prove him right, McDougall collected an armed force to battle his way to Fort Garry. He expected the English half-breeds to support his cause, since they remained independent of the métis, but they envisioned their lands as being torn up if fighting occurred, so they remained neutral. Former fur traders and other adventurers who felt little allegiance to any group or country joined McDougall, but they didn't exactly show enthusiasm for open warfare. In addition, many of these adventurers had lived among the Indians or the métis and showed a liking for the men McDougall wanted to attack. He hesitated to force his way to Fort Garry with such a questionable band of supporters. Instead, he sent a group to Winnipeg to investigate the mood of people there, and Riel's men took them prisoner.

By this time the Hudson's Bay Company showed little interest in controlling Rupert's Land. Considering the region abandoned by the company, Riel, on December 8, declared his Provisional Government to be the authority in the territory. The president of the government conveniently resigned, and the métis quickly elected Riel to succeed him. Ottawa sent officials to negotiate, inflating

94

Riel's ego, but these men undermined his position in secret talks with his less-enthusiastic followers. As a result, when he tried to get motions passed he met with defeat, something he could hardly tolerate. He flared up time and again and finally imprisoned officials who appeared to be his main opponents. Other officials later issued the métis an invitation to carry their List of Rights to Ottawa. This, to Riel's mind, amounted to recognition of his Provisional Government, so he released some prisoners and may have given orders to allow the rest to escape.

Unaware of the peaceful outcome of negotiations, hotheads decided to force the release of prisoners. They attacked but ended up as prisoners themselves. Riel immediately wanted to exhibit the authority of his government, to prevent any such unrest and opposition in the future. When an old enemy, Thomas Scott, stirred up further trouble, he provided Riel with a scapegoat. Apparently Scott received an unfair trial, during which no witnesses were allowed to speak in his defense. The court ordered him to be shot, on March 4, 1870, and most outsiders as well as many of Riel's followers considered Riel "guilty of murder." Many métis returned to their farms, leaving the head of the Provisional Government in a weakened position. Soon Rupert's Land became part of Canada and British soldiers headed west to ensure a peaceful transfer of power to properly elected officials. Riel, seeing that his support was dwindling and fearing that he would be tried for Scott's death, fled. The formation of Manitoba Province meant that roads and railroads would follow. The métis, with their List of Rights ignored, faced the necessity of adopting the pattern of life established by the newcomers or being driven from their own lands. Some immediately trailed west after Riel. Others, after trying to retain their individuality, also moved or adapted to "foreign" changes.

During the 1860's the Pacific coast of Canada gained numbers of settlers. But mountain ranges, such as the

Rockies, separated them from the rest of Canada. As a result western settlers had many contacts with Americans to the south. Officials in Ottawa saw the need to establish the province of British Columbia to ensure keeping it out of the hands of the United States. Many people of the region agreed, but they wanted a railroad to connect their region with the rest of the country. After they received the promise of a railway, British Columbia became a province in 1871.

Surveyors marking trails across the plains during the 1870's worried the Indians. The Canadian government promised to keep the railroad from creating hardships for the tribes, but in its struggle to finance the rail line the government cut back on the Indian food budget. Some tribes faced near-starvation, and many saw their lands sliced in two by the "steel snake" stretching across the prairies where buffalo once wandered freely. Chiefs lost faith in the Canadian government, especially when métis who had settled near them told disquieting stories of what had happened in Rupert's Land. As before, the half-breeds held their lands as squatters, but the builders of the Canadian Pacific Railway recognized no such claims if they stood in the way of the advancing track. When the métis sought land titles through Canadian officials, they met with vague replies or stalling tactics. Some métis had developed a business of transporting goods in oxcarts. Now freight cars would take much of their commerce from them.

Indian tribes had chiefs, but the métis seemed nearly leaderless. Louis Riel had become a teacher in Montana. The métis knew of his whereabouts, however, and asked him for help. During his exile from Canada, Riel had periods of insanity, but when the métis reached him he appeared to be all right. He lived in poverty, for which he blamed the Canadian government, but his desire to lead remained strong. After he returned to Canada, his behavior became odd. He lived on a diet of blood cakes and

96

claimed to have visions, but the métis and the Indians felt that this meant he had contact with God.

Riel wrote up the métis and Indian demands—reasonable requests for the most part. They would lessen the dictatorial position of the railway company and give the local people a chance to live in their natural ways. For answer, the Canadian government sent mounted policemen. In 1869, while troops had struggled across portages to reach Fort Garry, Riel had been able to negotiate with government agents. But in 1884 armed forces boarded a train in Manitoba and arrived to oppose him within a matter of days. Surprised and chagrined, he led the half-breeds on a series of irrational raids. They took prisoners, captured railway and government supplies, and encouraged the Indians to go on the warpath. Remembering how he had controlled Rupert's Land from Fort Garry, Riel decided to take Fort Carlton, in the heart of what is now Saskatchewan. Major L. N. F. Crozier commanded the fort. With only about fifty mounted police and a slightly smaller number of volunteer militiamen, he set out to teach the métis a lesson. Having underestimated their strength, he fled back to Fort Carlton with almost a fourth of his men dead or seriously wounded. The métis' rebellion in Rupert's Land had been nearly bloodless. The new uprising would be much different.

Raw Canadian troops went on the alert to move west, but the worst stretches between Ontario and Manitoba had not yet been connected by rail lines. Getting from Sudbury, Ontario, to Winnipeg in Manitoba still presented a time-consuming challenge. When no force arrived to retaliate for Crozier's defeat on March 26, 1885, Cree Indians under Big Bear massacred civilians and priests at Frog Lake, one hundred and fifty miles north and west of Fort Carlton. The Canadian Pacific, on the verge of bankruptcy, provided all the service it could manage—hoping to obligate the government to bail it out financially—and before the end of April poorly trained soldiers faced guerrilla bands of métis and Indians. In some early skirmishes, the soldiers made poor showings, but they quickly learned the rebels' tactics and adjusted their own style of fighting. Riel, who had established a provisional government, occupied Batoche, about twenty miles from Fort Carlton. Recognizing the difficulties of holding the town, which had no fort, he called for métis guerrillas and the two main Indian forces, under Big Bear and Poundmaker, to join his troops. The Canadian leaders had already seen the necessity of keeping rebel groups from teaming up, however, and few supporters reached Batoche. On May 12, the town fell to Major General Frederick Middleton, and Riel gave himself up, perhaps unable to find a means of escape. He was hanged.

Like the Indians in much of North America the métis had been forced to move by intruders—settlers, governments, and railroads. No suitable lands remained to which the half-breeds could escape. They developed their own schools and made some effort to keep their language and a few customs alive, but for the most part they resigned themselves to a new way of life. As so often proves to be the case, a minority group suffered.

In the nineteenth century, railroad builders seemed to think that nearly every village and town should be on a rail line. Cars, trucks, and buses later proved them wrong. So today road builders displace people and eliminate farmland in order to slap down one expressway after another.

11
COMPANY TOWN, COMPANY THUMB
Miners and Laborers

In the second half of the 1800's, successful mining companies bought one after another of the small coal, silver, copper, and other mineral claims across the United States and Canada. By 1890, for instance, the Colorado Fuel and Iron Corporation had grown into a powerful, statewide organization. Many mines existed in remote regions, where workers hammered together shacks to live in. The Colorado company and others recognized advantages to be gained by building their own communities. In these isolated company-owned mining towns, roofs leaked, windows refused to open unless they refused to close, floors might be of dirt, and the only running water was at a few taps sticking out of the ground or possibly at the nearest stream. Private, indoor toilets seldom existed. Bachelors and married men who left their families in more civilized communities shared dormitory rooms with dozens of other men and even shared beds where the demand for laborers outran the construction of accommodations.

In some towns men got falling-down drunk, pestered women on the streets, and knifed each other on Saturday night without losing their jobs as long as they went into the mines on Monday morning. Let them complain about living or working conditions, however, and they soon regretted it. Each company town had police, those known to the community and secret ones who listened for the griping of malcontents. Knowing how much unrest complainers could start, company owners removed them promptly. The miners often paid higher rents than the buildings, the times, and the wage scales warranted, and they had to shop at company stores—no others existed—where prices ran high. After feeding and clothing their families, men often lacked enough money to pay all the rent. They went into debt, hoping for a raise that would let them catch up on the arrears. To remove complainers, the company fired them and foreclosed on their shacks, throwing them out into the street. As vagrants having no employment, they faced the company police, who hustled them and their families out of town. This was known as sending them "down the canyon." Their names went to other mines and towns on a blacklist, and they seldom found other jobs. Foreclosure supposedly protected landlords from squatters who tried to gain illegal control of property. In a company town it became a weapon for keeping laborers in line with company desires.

Leaders who tried to live beyond the grip of big companies entered the scene. They endeavored to start unions, hoping to help laborers escape problems faced in communities controlled by corporations. As a result, company towns figured in some famous labor struggles. Homestead, Pennsylvania, a few miles up the Monongahela River from Pittsburgh, developed into a company town of Andrew Carnegie's great steel empire. In good times unskilled workers spent twelve hours a day in smoke-filled air to earn possibly two dollars a day. Skilled laborers fared better, receiving four to seven times that much for a day of eight or ten hours. During depressions the unskilled struggled for the same hours under the same lung-clogging conditions for perhaps ten cents an hour. Safety and protective equipment hardly existed. Wives had only slightly less smoke and grime to contend with in their homes than

100

their husbands faced in the mills. In Homestead, men sometimes bought houses, but by 1892 probably fewer than a hundred families owned their homes. A few large buildings provided apartments, and bachelors lived in rooming houses. In low-lying areas nearby, the poorest-paid workers lived in tents, lean-tos, and shanties, perhaps paying no rent at all and still barely managing to avoid starvation.

The United States entered a period of uncertainty in 1889, and by 1892 a recession plagued the country. Henry Clay Frick managed the Homestead operations for Carnegie, and he saw only the company's side to every argument. His solution to a decline in company profits was a cut in workers' wages. When Frick demanded that workers take reductions in 1892, the Amalgamated Association of Iron and Steel Workers fought his terms. As it turned out, most men who would receive large wage cuts belonged to the union, so it was a political as well as an economic move. After nearly half a year of talks, Frick decided they accomplished nothing. Carnegie had gone to visit his homeland, Scotland, and remained there, out of reach of the workers he supposedly wanted to treat fairly.

The Amalgamated union had concentrated on attracting skilled workers, turning its back particularly on Slavs and Negroes. As a result, its membership numbered less than a thousand even after negotiations started, and it made a special drive to lure in new members. As union and other workers became more belligerent, Frick had a high wooden fence topped with barbed wire built around the mills. This forced laborers to enter and leave through gates—like criminals, some thought. Yet they remained at their jobs, knowing the slack times made their chances poor for finding work elsewhere. When rumors spread of possible foreclosures on families behind on rent or mortgage payments, some men concealed their discontent. A few joined the union, hoping it would save their jobs and houses, while others dropped out of it for fear membership

101

would cause them to lose what they had.

Before the union could call a strike, Frick and his associates planned a lockout. They kept out whatever laborers they considered undesirable, mainly union members and other agitators. In secret, Frick called on the Pinkerton National Detective Agency to supply him with three hundred guards. They were to arrive in boats and land inside the fenced area so they could be deputized as sheriffs before they faced the furious laborers locked out of the mills. However, word reached the Homestead families of Frick's maneuvers. This caused such fury among all laborers that Frick fired everybody on July 2 and closed all plants. He probably wanted to give everyone a taste of unemployment and assumed he could easily hire back all the nonunion help needed to operate the mills when he felt the time had arrived. He held off on foreclosures, not wanting to drive men away, but he allowed tales of dispossession to circulate, thinking fear could be his ally.

Outside the fence, workers formed a ring of pickets prepared to turn back scabs, called "black sheep" in those days. Coat pockets bulged with pistols. Men watched rail lines and roads, uncertain of how the Pinkerton agents would arrive. When word came that Carnegie plants in Boston and Chicago had lined up laborers for shipment to Homestead, unrest increased. Deputy sheriffs from Pittsburgh never got inside the fence but were sent back to the city by the pickets. Children, who had been allowed to play in the streets or playgrounds of Homestead, were kept closer to home.

The Pinkerton agency had rounded up whatever free men it could hire in a hurry, from bums to college students with insufficient funds to return to school. It put them into ill-fitting agency uniforms, and 316 of them came up the Monongahela on barges converted into metal-plated troop carriers. Homestead workers watched the river as well as the roads and depots and sounded the alarm before dawn on July 6. Some laborers opened fire on the barges.

Although this did little damage, it frightened the agents, who had understood they would guard company property rather than fight. The few longtime Pinkerton hands in charge had trouble preventing panic. Before the Pinkerton men could leave the boats, angry workers stormed the fence, broke it down along one weak stretch, and raced to line the bank above the landing spot.

Contradictory stories exist. According to some, firing broke out when the Pinkerton recruits started ashore. It received an immediate answer from the barges. Other stories say eight Pinkertons started ashore on a wide gangplank. One laborer stepped forward to protest, and the agents shot him before he could speak. In any case, in a morning of warfare several men on both sides lost their lives or were wounded. By afternoon, a stalemate existed. About three hundred guards remained trapped in one barge, while the laborers took occasional shots at the boats from behind barricades of scrap metal and lumber. As inactivity allowed their tempers to cool, the workers finally agreed to allow the Pinkerton agents to give up their arms and come ashore. They were to be marched to the depot and put on a train for immediate departure, but they had not gone far before laborers, women, and children started slapping, kicking, and stoning them. Workmen trying to protect the Pinkertons also received blows before they finally found refuge in a theater. Again the passage of hours produced a calming effect, and between midnight and dawn of July 7 the surviving hired guards reached a waiting train and departed for Pittsburgh. They had taken part in one of the bloodiest episodes of American labor relations. Later judgments blamed the workers for starting the shooting.

After quiet had returned to Homestead, the governor of Pennsylvania finally ordered state militia to the area. Frick allowed the soldiers to take charge before he rebuilt the fence and ferried new workers up the river. He intended to give these scabs on-the-job training for producing the products of the Homestead plants, but he really expected to get most of the old workers back before long. With black sheep safely inside "Fort Frick," where they lived in tents, Frick thought the unemployed men outside would return meekly. To his surprise none of them came crawling in. As a warning, Frick threw a few families and bachelors out of their homes, apartments, and rooms. The company leases permitted this even in cases of paid-up rents. When the workers remained strong in their determination to resist, Frick stepped up the program of dispossession, and by the end of July nearly a hundred evictions had been made. No force proved necessary to make the unemployed workers move. They went willingly though dejectedly rather than return to work. Wagons trundled weeping families to the depot or into Pittsburgh, while people without resources begged in the streets of Homestead until other families assisted them. The largest number of evictions came on July 30, a drizzly day that grew stormy as it progressed. About noon, rain pounded the area and people scurried about to throw covers of various sorts over furniture standing in the streets or bumping along in open wagons. Many household furnishings fell apart after standing in the rain for hours.

As soon as houses or rooms became vacant, scabs moved in, with the aid of soldiers if strikers stood in the way. In addition, new construction to enlarge the company town had started. Frick obviously expected to win. Some laborers began to fear they had acted too hastily, especially as the union ran short of funds to help them. Even after a would-be assassin shot him twice in the neck, Frick refused to bow to their demands. Although evictions had stopped, starvation forced one family after another to move away. Stores refused further credit but went bankrupt because the families lacked money.

Little by little the growing band of black sheep turned out steel and other products, and the Carnegie enterprises had fortunes behind them. They could survive longer than the unemployed laborers. Sympathy strikers at other Carnegie locations, seeing their jobs filled by scabs, either rioted and landed in jail or lost their compassion for the Homestead families and returned to their jobs on a nonunion basis. By the end of August, a trickle of Homestead strikers lost courage and seeped through the fence to take up their old jobs at lower wages. Cuts had been made in the number of soldiers on guard, and deputy sheriffs now had a large responsibility for order. They had a way of disappearing rather than appearing when a scuffle or brawl developed. A scab's property might catch fire, but the danger of setting the whole company town ablaze prevented much of this activity. A few black sheep feared for their lives and left, while others found the stifling, dangerous conditions of work more than they cared to face. But for every man who departed, two or three more arrived. Sickness broke out among the new workers not accustomed to laboring in temperatures well above 100° F., yet the furnaces flamed and smokestacks poured their soot over the company town.

In September a grand jury considering the events of July 6 handed down indictments for murder, conspiracy, and rioting against 167 laborers. This frightened more workers into asking for their old jobs back. During the trials, wives swore the men had been home in bed on the morning of the riot, and all went free. At the end of September the grand jury, perhaps with prodding from Frick, had thirty-five union men arrested for treason. This frightened some leaders into slipping away, but none who faced trial were found guilty. Laborers in their turn charged Frick and his associates with causing the riot and conspiring to reduce wages, but no convictions resulted.

After the trials ended, harassment of scabs resumed. Even as late as December some nonunion men were poisoned, but before that, the strike had petered out. By the second half of November the union went bankrupt and could no longer help the laborers, most of whom gave up and returned to work. Only a few union leaders refused to ask for their old jobs back. A blacklist carried the names of union members who would not be rehired, and these had to seek work with companies outside Carnegie's influence.

Two years later another major dispute involved the company town of Pullman, a suburb of Chicago. There the Pullman Palace Car Company produced Pullman cars for railroads. Workmen reported having a feeling of being completely under George M. Pullman's thumb. The houses, lots, stores, churches, and everything else in town except personal clothing and some furniture belonged to the company. Laborers outside the town frequently envied those living in Pullman, while those inside often envied those living freely elsewhere. Pullman residents had to rent. Many wished they could buy their lots and homes, achieving a sense of really belonging. It hardly helped their dispositions to see workers in nearby Chicago paying lower rents, lower gas bills, lower water bills, and lower prices at stores. Yet they had one advantage that made them afraid to move. Residents of Pullman, Illinois, were the last laid off when times proved bad and the first rehired when business improved.

As early as 1885, the New York *Sun* reported, "The people of Pullman are not happy and grumble at their situation even more than the inhabitants of towns not model are accustomed to do. They say all this perfection of order costs them too much in money and imposes upon them an intolerable constraint. . . . They secretly rebel because the Pullman Company continues its watch and authority over them after working hours."

Thomas W. Heathcoate, a Pullman workman, revealed that "If I only had nine dollars coming to me, or any other amount, the rent would be taken out of my pay. . . . I have seen men with families of eight or nine children to support crying there because they got only three or four cents after paying the rent. . . . I have been insulted at that

106

window time and time again by the clerk when I tried to get enough to support my family."

The poor times of 1892 led to worse times the following year. Pullman cut wages, but rents, gas and water rates, and prices in stores remained the same. The laborers recognized some reasons for reducing wages, but they insisted their living expenses needed to be lowered simultaneously. The company continued to pay dividends to stockholders without cutting them, making the workers even more certain that they received unfair treatment. A committee called on Pullman to present their grievances, and soon afterward certain of its members found themselves dismissed. In protest on May 11, 1894, two thousand members of the new American Railroad Union struck.

Pullman and his executives said they anticipated no violence, yet welcomed a large detail of police from Chicago. The workmen feared that other Pullman shops could fill orders and prolong the strike, so the union decided to boycott every Pullman product on the rails if the company refused to arbitrate. The boycott went into effect on June 26, soon affecting more than a dozen railroads and idling five thousand men. At one yard, fifty switchmen halted a locomotive, drew a revolver on the engineer, and forced him to leave fourteen cars of perishable goods on a siding. The threat of violence mounted. When the company tried to transfer its main operations to St. Louis, the union called out the workers there. Within a few days forty thousand laborers had left their jobs. A hundred carloads of bananas rotted on sidings between New Orleans and Chicago. Police rushed here and there, wherever a threat of violence occurred. As at Homestead, the union found difficulty in caring for the strikers. By late June its relief committee had money to buy food for only two more days, and *The New York Times* reported, "destitution and starvation threaten the strikers." Eventually at least ten thousand of the thirteen thousand residents of Pullman needed assistance. Fear of starvation forced families to move, but most felt they lacked enough funds even to get out.

When union activities interfered with mail service, the strikers weakened their cause. Federal troops arrived, and within a few days leaders of the railroad union were arrested. Seeing defeat ahead, railroad union officials offered to end the strike if workers would be rehired without prejudice, but Pullman rejected the offer. The company lined up nonunion help and in August reopened the Pullman plant. In panic some strikers returned to work, bringing an end to the official walkout. But many workers remained firm. On August 10, the Pullman spokesmen said the company needed housing for new workers and would apparently have to find it by dispossessing all strikers behind on their rent. This could affect about three thousand families, which would easily accommodate the one thousand new men coming in as scabs. The company awaited results, but few workers returned. On the thirteenth, the company announced that eviction papers were being drawn up. When newspapers found fault with the company for its cruelty, an official said the ejection plan had been given undue and inaccurate coverage in the press. The company, according to the spokesman, had too many other matters under consideration to think about throwing people out into the streets. What he should have said was, the threat of eviction had served its purpose. Most strikers had decided to come back to work. The company did point out, however, that "in cases deemed proper by the company, notice will be given." In other words, the officials intended to drive out strike leaders and uncontrollable troublemakers.

The United States Government made a strike study, led by Carroll D. Wright, Commissioner of Labor, and decided a worker should use no more than one fifth of his pay for rent. Each man should be allowed to own his home and lot, which would go far toward making happy laborers. Cities should develop their rapid-transit systems and offer service at low rates so workers could live farther from work and have more freedom and privacy. This indicates that the committee wanted to eliminate company towns of the sort existing in Homestead, Pullman, and mining areas. Between World War I and World War II the decline of the company town came about. The mass production of motor vehicles within a workingman's budget helped make this possible. And buses allowed cities to open new transportation routes without the high cost of laying streetcar tracks or digging subways. Individuals no longer had to live within walking distance of work.

12
ENGINEERING
A MOVE

TVA and
St. Lawrence Seaway

In the first decade of the twentieth century President Theodore Roosevelt supported the idea of preventing serious floods through man-made controls. The idea originated before his time, but he made a particularly strong effort to promote it. His proposal to harness the Tennessee River, however, needed more backers than he found. During World War I a hydroelectric dam was started in Alabama where a series of rapids, known as Muscle Shoals, made navigation of the Tennessee River difficult. Completed in 1925, the dam proved useful, especially for supplying electricity to nearby nitrate plants, but for years congressmen failed to agree on a program to control other sections of the river. Finally, in 1933, they passed the Tennessee Valley Authority Act.

Along the Tennessee River, farmers plowed the land or grazed their livestock. Other families had settled nearby and had opened stores or filling stations to do business with the farmers. Engineers preparing to harness the river had to take farms, homes, villages, roads, and railroads all into consideration. Where homes and towns stood lower than the levels to which waters would rise in man-made lakes, planners had to relocate people. With passage of the TVA Act in 1933, people had to move whether they wanted to or not. Marshall Wilson headed the "family removal division." Although such work was new to him, he read about what had been done earlier in New York and Massachusetts where reservoirs to supply water to New York City and to Boston had displaced families.

Problems arose that had not caused trouble before. Wilson had to deal with segregation. Whites usually refused to accept blacks in their communities, and many blacks objected to the arrival of newcomers who would compete for available jobs. In the course of its 650 miles the river flowed through a variety of soils. Soils that were clogged with clay barely allowed families to scrape out a living, and TVA officials tried to relocate such farmers on better, albeit fewer, acres. Often people objected to accepting less land than they gave up. It seemed desirable to pay them for their land according to its value and then help them to find another farm worth the same money, regardless of size. As soon as families had money in their hands, they thought of things they had always wanted. Wilson and his assistants had to help them immediately or the money was spent before new land could be found. It proved safer to find the new farm and obtain rights to it before letting a family have the money for their old place. People with debts and mortgages presented special problems. In addition to helping to settle these, TVA officials tried to move people during logical periods. Farmers could best be moved in early spring before they planted seeds or in the fall after they harvested crops. Although most farm families fared well in the moves, a survey later disclosed that one out of five was dissatisfied.

Moving a town presented special problems. Perhaps neighbors wanted to stay together, but locating empty houses side by side in a similar town might be impossible. A family with the only dry-goods store in a town being flooded hardly appreciated having to move to where competition existed. And people living at a well-traveled intersection certainly complained when they were placed at a crossroads where few cars passed. Sometimes only part of a town needed to move, which could create bitterness. Why couldn't the dam be a few feet lower so that nobody would have to move, or a few feet higher so everybody had to go? About a thousand people lived in the coal-mining town of Caryville, Tennessee, where rising waters would flood only the lower section. The TVA relocated as many families as possible on higher ground in the same town, allowing them to remain in familiar surroundings and to keep their jobs in whatever mines were not flooded. To help make certain they remained happy, the TVA provided new assets, such as a small park, to make Caryville more pleasant. Even then residents grumbled until the lake crawled up the hill and stopped just short of their doorsteps. After that the beautiful lakeside setting attracted new residents and many tourists, turning the town into a lively and profitable place.

The TVA officials wanted to relocate many people in completely new situations. These would be trained as laborers for the dams and other projects related to overhauling the Tennessee Valley. In October 1933 one of the first projects was started, Norris Dam on the Clinch River, a tributary of the Tennessee. Nearby, about twenty miles north of Knoxville, the government experimented with creating a town. The TVA purchased nearly five thousand acres, on which it erected homes, a school, farmers' market, recreation hall, hotel, and bus station. To provide an industrial section, it built shops related to work on the dam at the edge of town. When the work ended, these would give way to new industries attracted to the area. The dam would supply cheap electric power for homes and industrial plants. Estimates said the community could be created for $3,000,000, perhaps less. It received the name Norris, after Senator George W. Norris, who played a major part in getting the TVA Act passed.

In February 1934 the government started the first of 346 cement-and-cinder-block houses—small ones with

112

four rooms and larger ones with five. The TVA thought that it could build the smaller ones for less than $1,000 apiece because the houses would be basically the same and workers could put them together rapidly once they had constructed the first two or three. However, the planners had been thinking in terms of local wages. When work started, the government said workmen had to be paid government construction wages, and the price of each dwelling immediately rose. In addition, work progressed at roughly the same rate on the later houses as it did on the first ones. Once moved into the dwellings, families discovered them to be rather small. Soon signs of deterioration showed. The lack of eaves allowed water to run down the sides of houses, causing discoloration at the least and pitting and cracking at the worst. As the houses settled they developed cracks, and winds whined in when the frames of windows and doors became loose. Obviously, better houses had to be built, and the cost of creating the town went above $3,500,000.

Every house had a garden plot, and on the outskirts the TVA set up a beef cattle farm, a dairy farm, and a general produce farm. Unfortunately, the land turned out to be poor and the farmers' market became a drugstore. The school provided a variety of vocational studies for youngsters, hoping to keep them from returning to the subsistence farming their parents had previously known. And the adults learned various crafts, such as basket making, weaving, and pottery making. Many men studied blueprint reading, mechanical drawing, and electrical repair. All these projects looked forward to the time when the dam would be completed and would require only a small maintenance staff.

Some families described the town as dull and moved to Knoxville, since they could drive from there to their jobs at the damsite without difficulty. With everybody, even a soda jerker, receiving government-scale wages, everything proved expensive. Even electricity, despite the new

113

dam, wasn't cheap. All homes had been equipped electrically to take advantage of the inexpensive power, so they proved relatively expensive to maintain. A number of people decided they could live more economically elsewhere and moved out. After the dam was finished in the spring of 1936, many other families moved away. After all, how many blueprint readers and electrical repairmen did one town need? New industries failed to come to Norris. At that time a government lease carried a clause stating that the owner could reclaim the property on thirty days' notice. No firm wanted to start a factory without knowing that it could occupy the land for years or decades. The town shrank. It looked as though Norris might become the first cement-and-cinder-block ghost town in history.

In time the families of Knoxville discovered that Norris had assets—an attractive valley setting and nearby Norris Lake for recreation. They started coming during the summer for weekends or vacations. Word spread and visitors from farther away arrived. Now that automobiles were improved, people found they could commute from Norris to their jobs while living in the more peaceful, pleasant surroundings. The town began to fill up once more.

In the early 1940's the TVA experimented with wooden-frame houses put together on an assembly-line basis. For use near dam-construction sites and defense-work locations, these could be built at the rate of three a day. All were identical, but people added individuality by decorating and painting and by planting trees, bushes, or flowers. They proved much more satisfactory than the cabins of subsistence farmers in Alabama and Tennessee, yet families objected to moving, afraid they couldn't adjust to new ways of life. One family still did laundry in an old three-legged iron pot over a smoky fire. As a result, most of the women of the family had eye trouble, but they feared houses with electrical appliances. And would there be a place for the spinning wheel on which the mother produced thread? A small farm with an old but serviceable

114

house finally satisfied the family and they moved. When the story reached the press, some journalists wrote as if sections of the South still lived in another era, unaware of modern times. In truth most people used old furnishings and out-of-date appliances because they couldn't afford newer ones.

Mr. and Mrs. James Randolph and their seven children lived near the site of Norris Dam. Every few weeks an agent tried to get them to move, but Mrs. Randolph refused to leave the weatherworn cabin with its two small rooms. The trouble—Mrs. Randolph wasn't one for talking —seemed to be that she had moved too many times already. And other land had been worse. In many places farms along the river offered fine soil. The river carried topsoil from higher places and deposited it in low-lying areas during floods. This bottomland, as it is called, provided excellent fields. Though the Randolph property wasn't all that good, they had known worse places. Mrs. Randolph insisted that she would not leave their fifteen acres.

As Norris Lake spread across the fields, the Randolphs watched the water approach without alarm. About once each spring, they had seen floodwater slosh up the small hill toward their cabin. Mrs. Randolph failed to understand that these waters would reach higher than any before. She laughed to see the family pig wallowing at the edge of the lake when it reached the Randolph farm. About sixty chickens pecked at insects driven ahead of the slow-moving flood.

On January 18, the driveway disappeared underwater. Mrs. Randolph nodded her head and admitted that this might be slightly worse than most other times. She went about her work as usual, although this had become somewhat difficult because she now had all seven children, Mr. Randolph, and many of the chickens underfoot. She couldn't very well send the family out to work or play now that the land was flooded. More chickens came in as the

115

water reached the step. The sound of splashing brought the family to the door to watch two trucks plow slowly through the water covering the driveway. As the vehicles stopped, Mr. Wilson gave orders and workers with him began capturing the chickens and splashing after the pig. Without giving the Randolphs time to object, one man started reading an eviction notice, while Wilson and another man went into the house and started bringing out the movable furniture. The man reading the eviction notice raised his voice to be heard above the squealing of the pig and the squawking of hens. Mrs. Randolph said that high waters didn't frighten her, as she'd seen them every year. "We went to bed and slept as usual." But workmen took her by the arm as if to treat her as they had treated the chickens and the pig. Rather than be tied up in the back of a truck, she waded to the cab of one and angrily took a seat.

A moment later, Mrs. Randolph heard the crackle of flames. Having taken out everything movable, the men had set fire to the house to keep it from floating down to crash against the dam. Wilson lodged the Randolphs at a nearby poor farm, and a social worker took Mr. Randolph farm-hunting. They found a place with a nicer house than the one from which the Randolphs had been evicted, but Mr. Randolph feared that his wife would refuse it. In silence she looked it over and debated. Finally she nodded, and the Randolphs moved for the last time.

As the TVA work progressed, individuals and companies continued to object to the project. They worried about the cost. They fretted that roads, railroads, and certain large manufacturing plants would have to be relocated. It especially bothered people that the TVA might go into competition with local electric companies. Seldom did it seem to bother them that individuals would be driven from their houses or that whole towns might have to relocate. The subsistence farmer and small homeowner didn't have lobbyists to stir up a fuss in Washington as

116

manufacturers, railroads, and public utilities did. Even so, the work proceeded. At the time Norris was built, newspapers carried stories debating the advisability of allowing the government to become a major landlord. At times the government wished that it had listened to these last arguments. In 1948 it auctioned off the town, which was bought by a private corporation for a little more than $2,000,000, and the corporation eventually sold it to the residents.

For a quarter of a century the Tennessee Valley has escaped the destructive floods of the years before the TVA. In general, the people who had to move found themselves better off than before. The people being moved as well as the people wanting them to move were considered, and the results are believed successful.

Other such projects have been considered in various places. Certain ones involving beautiful canyons of the West have so far been defeated, for they would eliminate scenic wonders and help commercialize some of the few remaining naturally wild areas of the United States. What will happen in a decade or so cannot be predicted. An eastern project that eventually received approval was the St. Lawrence Seaway. Here again, towns and individuals had to be relocated. Roughly nine thousand people—about three fourths of them Canadian—found themselves forced from their homes to make this engineering accomplishment possible.

The families involved had clearer warnings than many of those in the Tennessee Valley. Two decades had passed, and far more people owned radios and telephones and bought newspapers. Yet few families were really prepared, and some objected to moving when the time came. An old woman in New York State kept her shotgun handy, awaiting the day authorities would try to send her away. They came, and she held them at a distance for hours until they convinced her of the logic in moving. When bulldozers arrived at Iroquois, a village in Ontario, townspeople

117

and farmers faced them with guns and forced them to turn back. They could not stop the Seaway work, but at least the families of Iroquois saved some of their century-old houses and other buildings. Officials agreed to move the structures intact to a location about a mile back from the river.

Indian reservations on both sides of the river lost part of their lands. Although treaties existed to protect Indian properties, government officials felt these treaties could be changed in view of unusual circumstances. But the day had passed when Indians lacked help in high places. Lawyers forced the governments to pay higher prices for reservation acres than the first offers provided. One Indian farmer refused to move even when digging equipment ran trenches to his front and back doors. With the work at a complete standstill, officials paid him several times more than the amount originally offered.

The success of the Seaway is still being debated, but most opinions consider it worth the expense and trouble involved. Families generally benefited. Land prices along the river had remained low for years because people feared that the project would be undertaken. As a result, the prices paid exceeded those the landowners ordinarily could have expected. Young people had moved away rather than wait to be driven out, but stability has now returned to the area. House-moving equipment, developed since the early days of the TVA, saved many structures, making it unnecessary for numbers of elderly people to adjust to new homes.

13
CONCENTRATION CAMPS
Nisei

Japanese immigration to the Western Hemisphere began in 1884 when unskilled laborers moved to Hawaii to work on sugarcane plantations. Many later went to California, where they found ready-made prejudices awaiting them. The Chinese had preceded them, arriving during the California gold rush of 1848. As gold strikes diminished, prospectors became frustrated and frustration led to anger, directed especially toward anyone with a "foreign" appearance. Why should "outsiders" be permitted to carry off American gold? All Orientals who followed the Chinese to North America have faced the hostility that started during the mid-1800's. The Japanese endured the discrimination, as the Chinese did, although some moved to Oregon, Washington, and British Columbia, where prejudice seemed less than in California. Many consoled themselves with thoughts of returning to the Orient as soon as they could save enough money to live there comfortably.

By the turn of the century about twenty-five thousand Japanese lived in the western part of the United States and another five thousand lived in Canada, but they were not all immigrants. Numbers of children had been born on United States and Canadian soil. Parents tried to keep children "Japanese" by retaining Oriental customs and by

119

educating them at home or in private schools. But adults can never completely stifle the natural curiosity of youngsters. Children became interested in the cultures around them and unconsciously picked up new attitudes and manners. As decades passed, new generations picked up more American ways and began to look upon Canada or the United States as home.

Japan's invasion of China in the 1930's provided a setback for relations between Americans and Nipponese (in Japanese, the name for Japan is Nippon). Japanese Americans who sent money to Japan may have been helping needy relatives, but they came under suspicion of financing the war. Non-Orientals suspected private Japanese schools of training future soldiers and diplomats for the spreading imperialism of Japan. Bilingual Americans read the West Coast's Japanese-language newspapers to see if they contained subversive propaganda. The outbreak of World War II and the ease with which submarines secretly approached North America made coastal communities extremely nervous.

On December 7, 1941, Japan launched a surprise offensive against the United States by attacking Pearl Harbor. The attack came without assistance from an Oriental fifth column, yet every person of Japanese ancestry became a suspect. Authorities imposed curfews to keep Japanese aliens and Japanese Americans confined to their homes after dark. Secret Japanese societies received orders to disband, for some of these, such as the Black Dragon Society, showed signs of militarism. Army officers ordered people of Japanese, German, and Italian descent to move away from naval yards, refineries, and certain factories of importance to the war effort. But these measures failed to provide the feeling of security sought by large portions of the West Coast population.

On February 19, 1942, the President of the United States gave the Army authority to remove all civilians from areas considered strategically important during

120

World War II. Franklin D. Roosevelt's Executive Order No. 9066 gave military commanders the power to "prescribe military areas" and to exclude from them "any or all persons." General John L. De Witt, Commander of the Western Defense Command, responded to pressures from the non-Japanese populace to call Washington, Oregon, California, and part of Nevada strategic and to relocate the Japanese in them to other states. One cooperative group of Japanese descent voluntarily started east almost immediately, but Governor E. P. Carville of Nevada said they would be placed in concentration camps if they came into his state. Governors of several other states said they would not guarantee safety to any refugees of Japanese descent. Officials then recognized the need for arranging placement of the evacuees. The War Relocation Authority, headed by Milton Eisenhower, quickly threw together internment camps—ten eventually—in various states as far east as Arkansas. Some of these had previously served as Civilian Conservation Corps or military camps and lacked provisions for handling women and children, while others mushroomed in the most desolate and undesirable desert and mountain regions imaginable. Japanese who left of their own accord sometimes found work as hands on inland farms and received permission to stay there instead of going to camps. And the University of California helped Japanese students to transfer to inland colleges and universities that would accept them so they could continue their studies.

This left tens of thousands of other Japanese Americans to be relocated. Although many genuinely frightened citizens sincerely thought they needed protection, others probably wanted to gain control of good land or successful businesses owned by the Japanese. Or they sought the removal of the hardworking Oriental competition. Some non-Orientals reported seeing lights blinking along nearly deserted shores, supposedly signals to submarines lying quietly in the darkness until coded messages told them to

121

send rafts ashore or to shell certain places. Investigations failed to verify these reports, and signals, if there had been any, could easily have been sent by German or Italian fifth columnists. On the night of February 23, a submarine did shell an oil refinery near Santa Barbara, California. About twenty shells hit the area but did only slight damage. Witnesses saw the vessel from the shore, a large, dark shape in the water, but could not identify it. It might have been German instead of Japanese. Its raid helped speed up the evacuation of Japanese, German, and Italian peoples from strategic areas, but only the Japanese had to go to camps. This unusual treatment of more than 100,000 Japanese had to result primarily from prejudice against a little-understood minority. The fact that Orientals often made little effort to be understood hardly justified host countries for making little effort to understand them.

In Hawaii people of Japanese descent made up about one third of the population. If there had been a need for internment camps, the Hawaiian Islands would have required them. Instead of confining the Japanese, Hawaiian officials allowed them to continue with their regular business and personal routines. A few who were suspected of questionable activities were arrested, including the head of the Japanese Chamber of Commerce. But in general the Hawaiian Japanese proved loyal to the United States and contributed to winning the war. Many Japanese served with distinction in the United States Armed Forces.

Canada placed only a small number of its Japanese population in guarded camps, all of them internees who showed signs of being dangerous. But officials did take control of Japanese fishing boats, closed Japanese schools, and declared a strip about a hundred miles wide along the British Columbia coast as an off-limits area. The out-of-bounds strip created a need to relocate about twenty thousand Japanese Canadians. About four thousand agreed to go east voluntarily and were allowed to do so, while work for about six thousand was found in road-building camps and on sugar-beet farms. To accommodate the others, government and military authorities hastily built towns or helped the Japanese bring old ghost towns back to life. In general, the Canadian Japanese suffered less personally and financially than their relatives to the south.

Fearing that the United States Government would disregard its promise of protecting their property, many Japanese sold homes, businesses, and other property in such haste that they suffered severe financial losses. Putting up "I am an American" signs on business establishments accomplished nothing. In time these disappeared, to be replaced by "Under new management" signs. Losses also occurred on which price tags could not be placed—the goodwill of neighbors, self-respect, and feelings of independence, of accomplishment, or of contributing to society.

The Japanese who had not voluntarily left restricted areas and coastal zones by the end of March faced compulsory evacuation by the military. This started in Washington on March 29, when 227 Japanese were removed from an island near the Puget Sound Navy Yard. In California, the first compulsory removals were all men, who went to a camp at Manzanar, California, to ready it for their families and other people who would follow. Those going in their own vehicles traveled in a convoy accompanied by highway patrolmen and military police in patrol cars and jeeps. The rest went by train. One of the first arrivals at Manzanar reportedly said, "This is a wonderful place. We didn't expect such fine treatment." Later arrivals proved less enthusiastic. Generally, the Japanese said they received courteous treatment from the officers and guards who moved them. By early June the removal had been completed, leaving near the coast only Nipponese who were considered absolutely unreplaceable in important jobs.

The camps had a variety of discomforts. Most accommodations consisted of barracks rather than houses, and partitions between rooms did little to confine the sounds of daily living. Cots offered thin mattresses or straw ticks, and for weeks some families had to use suitcases as substitutes for dressers and cupboards. A family of eight might have only two or three chairs. In freezing winter temperatures and on blistering summer days, during snowstorms and dust storms, people had to go to community toilets. Near each camp stood a military compound for soldiers who acted as guards, and another small area nearby provided headquarters for War Relocation Authority personnel. Even under more satisfactory conditions trouble would have broken out from time to time. Camps soon acquired jails, and jails acquired prisoners. But most Japanese busied themselves improving their accommodations, building furniture, or planting and tending gardens. The War Relocation Authority officials tried to handle complaints, but for the most part the Japanese ran the camps themselves.

Once Allied forces gained the offensive in the Pacific and moved toward Tokyo, feeling against the West Coast Japanese decreased. On January 1, 1945, the internment order expired, and people from the camps could return to their old homes or find new ones. Before the war, nearly 90 percent of the Nipponese in the United States lived on the West Coast. Now a number of them moved east, especially to Chicago, and after they became settled only 70 percent of America's Japanese lived in the Pacific Coast states. Even fewer remained along the coast in British Columbia, while Toronto became a new center for them. The hardships of internment continued. Few Japanese could buy back the lands or the businesses they had owned before. Formerly independent Japanese had to work for other people or start new gardens and businesses on a small scale.

Prejudice faced them almost everywhere. Finding employers willing to hire them sometimes proved difficult, and wages frequently remained below those earned by other workers. Shopkeepers might refuse to sell them groceries or other necessities. Landlords told them no vacancies existed or offered them rooms, apartments, and houses at rents higher than other tenants had to pay. It took several years for the interned Japanese to return to what could be considered normal living. They never did return to certain of their old ways. After they left the camps, they either lacked the resources to start schools of their own or recognized the value of using public institutions. They published fewer Japanese-language papers and read more of the local publications in English. As a result, the Japanese came to feel a part of the whole community in which they lived, and the other citizens gradually accepted them as fellow Americans. Still, it would be shortsighted, even in the 1970's, to think that prejudices on both sides have entirely disappeared.

Children born since the relocation camps closed find that older people are reluctant to talk about their internee experiences. Some of the people who were adults at that time seemed to feel a sense of guilt, as though in a way it was their fault they had to go to the camps. As Ron Miyamura, a Buddhist priest of Japanese descent in Chicago, put it, they tried to become "two hundred percent Americans." Many of them remained as inconspicuous as possible after they gained their freedom. But numbers of Japanese who spent part of their childhood in the camps grew up with less fear about being in the public eye and have become prominent citizens of their communities. In the spring of 1971, Norman Mineta became the first Japanese American to win a mayoral race in a major United States city. As a child he lived for two years in a relocation camp, but as a man in his thirties he was elected mayor of San Jose, California. In the 1970's most people feel certain that there was no need for the camps and evacuation.

The internment undoubtedly caused emotional scars that have never healed. One man, after release from

125

confinement, reportedly said, "I am an American citizen . . . and I don't know Japan or what Japan stands for. . . . But I am going where I won't have to live on the wrong side of the tracks just because my face is yellow. I will find my future in the Orient." Other Japanese made new lives for themselves in the United States and Canada but had trouble forgetting the wartime restriction. In the book about his life in the United States, Daniel Okimoto, a second-generation Japanese American, tells of a Japanese who continued to have nightmares about his internment-camp experiences and to scream in his sleep for someone to let him out.

14
GONE, THE "LITTLE GRASS SHACK"
Bikini

During World War II, in the spring of 1944 American forces freed the northernmost islands of the Marshalls group from Japanese occupation. The cheerful, soft-spoken, easygoing islanders greeted the Allied servicemen with *"Yokwe yuk,"* which roughly means "Love to you." If they find Americans less lovable in the 1970's, it should surprise no one. Military officials decided the Pacific atoll of Bikini would make an excellent testing ground for nuclear weapons, so about 165 people had to move.

Military officers considered the Bikinians among the most backward islanders in Micronesia and assumed they would be satisfied on any atoll similar to their own, which they pronounce BICK-in-ih. The officials gave King Juda to understand that the use of his home atoll would result in "kindness and benefit to all mankind." Bikinians are among the kindest people in the world, so Juda and the twelve *alaps,* or elders, reluctantly agreed to move. The authorities located an uninhabited atoll, Rongerik, which appeared to be like Bikini. They took the Bikinians from their huts of bamboo poles interwoven with banana-tree and coconut-palm leaves and deposited them 115 miles to the south. Rongerik proved to be entirely different from Bikini. It provided about two thirds less agricultural area,

127

which meant far fewer coconut trees, and the coconut practically keeps Bikinians alive. Fish account for the rest of their diet, but poisonous varieties in the Rongerik lagoon made the people afraid to eat seafood from it. The military failed to watch after the welfare of the people, and day by day they grew more hungry. When a Navy ship finally visited them, a report led to some food being taken to Rongerik, but soon it was gone and Bikinians found themselves left alone and gradually facing starvation once more.

The authorities during this time busied themselves with preparing for and conducting the tests for which Bikini had been commandeered. Two blasts in 1946 sank or damaged dozens of out-of-date American and captured Japanese ships. In 1947 the officials took Juda to view Bikini from a distance, and he was surprised and pleased to find that it had survived the explosions. He wanted to bring his people back, but Bikini remained contaminated with radioactivity and the military had not yet finished using it. The visit served a useful purpose, however, for Juda called attention to the starving condition of the Bikinians. Embarrassed to have the world learn of this, the United States Navy brought Dr. Howard G. MacMillan, an agricultural specialist, to study the atoll. Some military officials thought the Bikinians went hungry purposely to force the United States to return them to Bikini. MacMillan reported otherwise. Rongerik had an unproductive soil, received almost no rain, and wasn't large enough to support many people. The Navy looked about for another deserted atoll and found one called Ujelang. After announcing that the Bikinians would be moved to it, the authorities discovered that other American officials had already chosen it as a home for people to be forced off Eniwetok, another Micronesian atoll wanted for testing purposes. After five months of further neglect the Bikinians were taken to Kwajalein, one of the largest islands of the Marshalls and one already serving the United States as a military base.

128

With each move, the people got farther from Bikini, which worried them. They believed ancestral spirits protected them. Because Rongerik had been a relatively short distance from Bikini by Pacific standards, they thought the spirits should have been able to locate them. But the fact that they nearly starved indicated otherwise, or so they thought. Now, still farther away, they feared that the spirits would never find them. Instead of planning to take them home, the officials located another place, the island of Kili, four hundred miles from Bikini. The Bikinians wondered if their ancestral spirits would give up searching for them. In November 1948, the Navy moved the Bikinians to Kili, and five months later reported them to be self-sufficient. In five months they hardly had time to get settled, let alone become self-supporting, and it seems possible that officials wanted to make their situation sound favorable to forestall a United Nations or other investigation. The United States supervises the islands and atolls of Micronesia as a Trust Territory for the United Nations. Only as long as the country held the trusteeship could it go on using Bikini and Eniwetok for military experiments.

The Bikinians were better off than they had been on Rongerik, but they had become even more unhappy. In addition to being farther away from the atoll of their ancestors, they now lived on an island. It offered more land area, being a solid mass, but the older Bikinians missed the lagoon, the center of every atoll. And the fact that the Navy now paid more attention to them still did not guarantee they would always have enough to eat. During one drought, when almost no plant produced edible fruits, nuts, or roots, the Navy dropped a ton of food on Kili. Food dropped by parachute sometimes drifted out to sea on the air currents and fed the fish instead of the Bikinians. So an attempt was made to "bomb" the island with food packages. Without parachutes to provide a "soft" landing, the crates smashed on the ground, scattering the food far and wide and demolishing or dirtying

129

most of it until it could not be salvaged. Much of it spoiled in the tropical heat before the Bikinians could even find it.

In 1954 scientists miscalculated and radioactive substances from a hydrogen-bomb explosion over Bikini rode across the Pacific on strong winds. Four or five hours later Rongelap, one hundred miles to the east, was hit by a "heavy snowfall" of fallout. The "blizzard" continued for about eleven hours, and the hundred or so inhabitants had to be rushed to a hospital on Majuro Atoll. Sixty-four of them received treatment for burns and radiation sickness. For three years they remained at Majuro for observation, but in 1957 they began going home in small groups. From time to time one or another person exposed to the radiation developed a nodule on the thyroid gland. Since other people failed to develop such lumps, the fallout exposure definitely deserved the blame. To be sure the people with nodules received the best of care, the Navy flew them to the United States for removal of the growths. In every case, the material cut away proved to be harmless.

After 1958 no more tests were held at Bikini. The atoll stood deserted, scarred but far from being demolished by the twenty-three devices exploded in its vicinity. Although the Bikinians still wanted to return, military officials gave their desires little consideration, assuming the atoll had served its last useful purpose for mankind. It appeared as dead as the moon. Weeks passed. Where soil had collected in cracks of the stonelike coral surface, spots of green began to show. Vines reached up from the fissures and crept across the islets and reefs. In the lagoon, a flash of color signaled the presence of a tropical fish. Whether it had survived the blasts or had come to the lagoon from the open ocean is uncertain. Coconut crabs crawled out of the lagoon and sought among the vines and shrubs for coconut trees to rob of nuts. Finding trees completely absent, they changed their diet to the vegetation available.

130

Scientists who returned marveled at the tough, tropical growth that covered the ground. When word of this reached the Bikinians, they renewed their requests to be allowed to go home, even though they had been paid $325,000 for the atoll. President Lyndon B. Johnson sympathized with their wishes and in 1968 promised they could return. He ordered the Secretary of Defense and other officials to make Bikini livable again. The Bikinians now numbered about 350, thanks to modern medical care. The first children born after the original move had become parents by this time.

Engineers determined the amount of radiation left at the atoll and found it to be less than in some occupied regions of the world. Work crews removed debris from Bikini and attacked the undergrowth with machetes and bulldozers, clearing strips to be planted with coconuts, pandanus, and bananas. To help with the planting, a small group of Bikinian men were brought back to the atoll in the early 1970's. For the first few years the food supply would be limited—the coconut palm requires several years to mature. In the meantime, the Bikinians would have to be looked after like handicapped children. The military planned to bring them home in small groups, taking at least until 1975 and perhaps longer before all would be living on Bikini once more.

As preparations went forward, medical teams continued to visit Rongelap to check the people who had been exposed to radiation. On one visit they found nineteen-year-old Lekoj Anjain feeling weak. He had been operated on a few years earlier for a thyroid nodule, but this time the doctors discovered that his white-blood-cell count was abnormally low. They flew him immediately to Bethesda, Maryland, for the most advanced leukemia treatment available at the National Institutes of Health, but on November 15, 1972, he died. He had been one year old when the fallout from Bikini "snowed" down on Rongelap, and now he had become the first fatality of that disaster.

Should the Bikinians go back to their atoll? The program to return them slowed down after Lekoj Anjain's death. Observations will continue, but it is uncertain as to when Bikinians will all be home on Bikini. Military officials want to keep Eniwetok as a base, which may mean that its original inhabitants will remain on Ujelang indefinitely. Soft-spoken, easygoing people made sacrifices—more than they bargained for.

15
DOMINOES OR CHECKERS?
Vietnamese

As World War II ended, Communist organizations increased their efforts to win control of countries in which they operated. France faced them in guerrilla warfare in Indochina, at the southeast corner of Asia, and from 1945 until 1954 endeavored to hang on to its colonies there. The cost in money, time, and manpower became too great. As the French withdrew, the United States and Britain attempted to provide support for a number of countries facing what some world leaders called civil wars and others branded Communist aggression. The fall of one country, it was feared, could lead to the fall of another, like dominoes standing on end, when one falls against another it causes a whole line to topple. Vietnam in particular became a country with which the United States increasingly involved itself. American helicopters with American pilots to fly them went to Vietnam, and in mid-1961 United States officers decided to provide additional equipment, planes, and personnel. In February 1962 they established the United States Military Assistance Command in Saigon, but General Paul D. Harkins, put in charge of it, promptly denied that it would mean the involvement of American combat troops.

Many people of South Vietnam, the non-Communist

half, had no quarrel with the Communists pushing down from the north. They wanted to be let alone to tend their rice paddies. If they fed the guerrillas or provided them with hiding places, they did so in the hope of keeping their crops or homes from being burned. They would do the same for South Vietnamese forces if they passed through, and for the same reason. Vietnamese officials and their foreign advisers wanted support from the farmers and devised plans for getting it. They would gather the peasants into hamlets, where they could be watched and where they could be "protected" from contact with the Communist guerrillas.

The Strategic Hamlet Program was to bring ten million South Vietnamese farmers into villages by the end of 1962. When few of them came voluntarily into the communities set aside for them, soldiers drove them from the land at gunpoint and placed them in the hamlet areas. Once there, they had to build their own houses and fortifications, although the military provided a concrete clinic and "town hall." American and British advisers saw this as a means of hampering the Communists, but Ngo Dinh Diem, president of South Vietnam, recognized it as a way to place millions of indifferent people under his political control. He put his brother Ngo Dinh Nhu in charge and assumed that his family would thereafter be in a position to win every election.

Each village was to have a school, which, in addition to making the people literate, would supply them with propaganda intended to make them anti-Communists. South Vietnamese officials gave so much consideration to the schooling that they neglected to provide some villages with adequate water supplies or a clinic staffed with competent medical personnel. Guerrillas overran a few settlements without difficulty. About a year after the first hamlet reached completion in March 1962, American, British, and South Vietnamese officials reconsidered the Strategic Hamlet Program. Under new plans the relocated

134

peasants received payment for property lost or damaged during their forced move into the hamlets, but the compensation proved small when divided among millions of people. It hardly "bought" their loyalty. At the advice of the United States, the propagandists changed their approach and tried to convince the relocated people of how much more satisfactory their lives would become as they adjusted to village ways. But the people continued to show indifference. When a hamlet proved to be in an undesirable location, the authorities forced the people to a new place and burned the old one to keep it from benefiting the Communists. Some weary peasants feared they would be shifted around like checkers for the duration of the war. Only about one in five of the hamlets ever became livable. Time and again guerrillas slipped through the ring of hamlets built around Saigon, capital of South Vietnam, and officials finally admitted to the failure of the Strategic Hamlet Program.

The United States increased its involvement in Vietnam. Bombing became a tactic used frequently as the 1960's progressed. As the North Vietnamese forces and guerrillas maneuvered to escape bombings, they sought refuge in villages, assuming that civilian centers would be spared. This forced the South Vietnamese officials and their supporters to seek new ways of moving neutral people out of the way. When the Nationalists, or anti-Communists, suspected that a Communist force hid in a village, they warned the residents to take what possessions they could and depart. Sometimes warnings came from a helicopter equipped with a public-address system. Or a plane might fly over and drop leaflets on which the warning was printed. A drawing of a house being blown to pieces, along with the people in it, would, it was hoped, carry the message to people unable to read, or else it would alarm them enough that they would show it to someone who could read the words for them. When the anti-Communist side felt it had provided sufficient warning, it bombed or shelled the village, trusting that the innocent people had left. After a village had been shattered and pockmarked with explosions, troops with bulldozers arrived. They hoped to level the area and bury alive any of the Vietcong, or Vietnamese Communists, untouched in caves dug under the houses. Before being allowed to return to start rebuilding, the villagers who had moved to safety would be warned to drive guerrillas away from their settlement in the future to keep a repeat of the destruction from being necessary. Residents of a village in a particularly troublesome area might not be granted permission to return and rebuild but would be transported to a less strategic location. Some people dejectedly moved to overcrowded cities too large to become targets for total annihilation.

The Communists also read the leaflets or heard the warning broadcasts. In some cases they dug shelters under the houses and hoped to survive the shells or bombs, but most of them left with the noncombatants. They found other communities in which to hide, for it would waste fighting time to help these people rebuild and struggle through a period of poverty while recovering. If a few did stay to help, they did it for propaganda purposes, trying to show that they were forces of construction as opposed to the Nationalist forces of destruction. If the anti-Communists returned with equipment and foodstuffs to help villagers rebuild and recover, any Vietcong remaining tried to get control of these supplies. Americans who advised total destruction of Communist-occupied settlements probably contributed hardships for innocent people rather than setbacks for the Vietcong.

After American forces withdrew from Vietnam, North Vietnamese and Communist troops pushed toward Saigon. In the spring of 1975 their drive gained momentum, and one province after another fell. What some of the farmers and villagers suffered at the hands of the victors may never be known, but fear of what might happen sent

136

hundreds of thousands of refugees flocking southward. Rumors of atrocities accompanied them. Considering that small children who had lost their parents might have no one to look after them and no way to care for themselves, the United States, Canada, Australia, and Great Britain launched airlifts to fly out hundreds of orphans. The flights started early in April and removed several thousand supposedly homeless and parentless youngsters from the war-ravaged country. As it turned out, some officials and rich Vietnamese took advantage of the flights to send their children to safety with relatives and friends abroad, but this could have been expected. They had been taking advantage of their allies since the French left Indochina. And as long as they didn't crowd out any orphans, it probably didn't matter.

Soon after plans for the flights became public some psychiatrists of the world expressed doubts about the wisdom of this forced relocation of orphans. Although most of them would be adopted in their new homelands, they would face problems of adjustment and would eventually encounter prejudice. Particularly after the novelty of their arrival wore off, doctors feared, they might have upsetting experiences. Whereas adoptions prove most satisfactory when the foster parents sincerely want to answer the needs of a child, psychiatrists wondered how many Vietnamese orphans were being taken to answer momentary needs of the adults. Most efforts to make the Vietnamese move, for whatever reason, had turned out unsatisfactorily. Would the orphan venture be another mistake?

Not all Americans proved blind to the likelihood of failure in the efforts to relocate Vietnamese farmers for strategic purposes. Reporters and even some military officers who visited hamlets could see how bitterly the local people resented being forced to move. One *New York Times* reporter visited the village that had been established as a showplace to represent all the villages. The occasion was an inspection by Ngo Dinh Nhu, and the reporter noticed a definite lack of enthusiasm on the part of the villagers. Young men in uniform were the main welcomers, but they had no choice. In general, the people appeared depressed and disheartened. When high officials weren't around to overhear, they told the reporter that they had to work about two months without pay to fortify the hamlet, and their families didn't have enough to eat. They were forced to buy flags they didn't want and display them, and when somebody decided that the first ones were the wrong size they had to buy a whole new set and weren't reimbursed for the old ones.

An observing American general said, "We can put ten thousand miles of barbed wire round the hamlets . . . but until we . . . give a better deal to the peasants we are never going to win this war." If many orphans eventually want to return to Southeast Asia, it could indicate that efforts to bring them peace also fell short.

16

THE SLUMS ARE
ALWAYS WITH US

Urban Renewal

The shocked residents of North Williamsburg, a section of Brooklyn, New York, learned in 1969 that their homes had been condemned and were to be destroyed. If they had occupied unpainted, dilapidated "firetraps" and "eyesores," the news might have proved less startling, but they lived in modestly substantial houses. An investigation revealed that an adjoining factory wanted their property in order to expand. The plant hired about five hundred people and expected to add an additional three hundred to its payroll if it could undertake a development program. If not, it would move to New Jersey to find more space. When the city officials envisioned the disappearance of the business taxes paid by the company and the income taxes paid by its employees, they felt desperate. But when they envisioned the additional taxes that would be paid by three hundred more workers, they sought a way to hang on to the factory. Economics, overriding humane considerations, led them to their decision, and about ninety families were to be thrown out of their dwellings. The largest number of people to be pushed aside were Polish, a minority in the city. Most of the rest were Slavs and Italians. Although many Italians live in the various boroughs of the city, even they constitute a minority.

City officials refused to meet with the residents, so the families hired a lawyer. He argued that the forced move was illegal on grounds of being for financial gain rather than for city improvement or urban renewal. The city wouldn't listen. Some of the residents saw opportunities for moving to satisfactory accommodations elsewhere and left, thus weakening the position of those who stayed. Even so, those remaining continued to fight. By mid-March 1973 about forty families still lived in twenty-two of the dwellings. After the state supreme court refused to set aside the condemnation, the residents received notice to be out by the end of April or face forcible removal.

Since legal action accomplished nothing, the people tried an illegal move. At eight o'clock on the morning of April 6, about forty women rushed onto the Brooklyn-Queens Expressway and sat down near the north end of the Kosciuszko Bridge in front of oncoming traffic. They blocked all three lanes leading into New York, and traffic screeched to a halt. Cars were soon lined up for blocks, waiting for the human blockade to move or be removed, and, before long, traffic was backed up for miles. The only thing louder than the swearing of drivers was the honking of horns. When police reached the scene, they tried to talk the women into clearing the southbound lanes. Talking gave way to arguing and, finally, shortly before nine o'clock, to more forceful tactics. Eighteen of the protesters were arrested before the group cleared the roadway.

Although the demonstration failed to save the homes, it brought the problem to statewide attention. Urban planners at Pratt Institute, a major university of Brooklyn, looked over the situation and showed how a compromise plan could save many of the houses. People sent letters of protest to city officials, especially to the mayor's office and to the Economic Development Administration. The EDA, involved in the decision to condemn the houses and move the people, feared the publicity and agreed to give the people better terms for their properties. But it refused compromise plans and continued to say the families had to vacate. April 30 arrived and a number of families still lived in the condemned houses. Spring turned to summer, and summer gave way to fall. The factory owners said they had to have the property if the city and state wanted them to stay. On October 15, police officers and city officials knocked on the doors of the homes where eight families continued to live. They led the people from their homes, almost dragging them when necessary, and two bulldozers ground into the area and battered down two of the houses while a growing crowd of people jeered and shouted protests.

As the affair quieted down, a city official in the EDA left his $32,000-a-year job to accept a position with the factory, and this new scandal shook several city offices. The official said he had had "nothing to do with the project at all" and had joined the EDA only in 1971, two years after the condemnations had been made. But he refused to say how much more his salary would be with the company than it had been with the city, and some of his former co-workers pointed out that he had been a city employee when decisions had been made to reject the compromises offered by Pratt Institute and others. At best, the clumsy handling of a delicate situation had given city improvement another blemish. At worst, a serious injustice had been committed.

Almost always some economic hardship figures in forced relocations for urban renewal projects, even though cities supposedly give people financial assistance at such times. Quite often psychological hardships result as well. No matter how poor a dwelling or neighborhood may be, it is home to the people who live in it. Elderly people, especially, may have lived there a long time and might find difficulty in adjusting to new locations. In the United States, families move on the average of every five years, but moving of one's own accord proves less upsetting than being made to do so. Since people with heavy mortgages or those who are buying into condominiums probably

141

move infrequently, the five-year average means that low-income families and those in substandard housing move even more often.

Sometimes protesters fare better than those of North Williamsburg. Boston undertook a project without making provisions for the people forced out. Quite commonly, planners decide on what will be done without consulting the families involved, but they usually make at least a token show of helping the displaced people find other permanent or temporary accommodations. The Boston residents grew so angry they staged a sit-in on a parking lot of the area. This led to arrests, but the next day even more people came, this time prepared to stay. They set up tents and hammered together shacks, dramatizing being left without living quarters. The police, deciding against further arrests, patrolled the area to prevent violence. Many of the people agreed that the area needed to be renovated, but they saw no reason why all the buildings should be knocked down at once when they could be replaced only a few at a time. Why couldn't people live in some of the old buildings until some of the new ones were ready for occupancy? Then families could make one move, into a new apartment, after which a few more of the old buildings could be torn down. After four days of camping on the parking lot, they won their point and disbanded.

In general the meek do not inherit new accommodations when being evicted from old ones. Relocation agencies sometimes make little effort to find facilities for people being forced out. Unless a family makes persistent and insistent inquiries about what is being done, a relocation board may allow a family to shift for itself. Minority groups are the ones most frequently affected, the ones most difficult to relocate satisfactorily, and the ones who receive the poorest service. If a family stays on in a building after the others have departed, it can be subjected to robberies, muggings, and possibly even to being burned out. Critics say that city, state, or federal authorities, depending on

142

what agencies are involved in an improvement project, should see to it that relocation work is carried out honestly, diligently, and promptly. If a relocation office proves neglectful, any government agency assisting with funds for the project should withhold that assistance until relocation services improve.

In past centuries, fires often eliminated the need for urban renewal, burning down the slums (and sometimes spreading to fine neighborhoods as well). Of course, hastily built shacks might replace for a time the buildings destroyed, but these usually gave way to new and better structures. City planning to do away with slums became of significance primarily in the twentieth century and particularly in the 1930's. Old people had to move in with their children, and families had to band together during the Depression, leaving houses and buildings empty—or nearly so. The people remaining could be shifted to vacant accommodations in other low-rent areas, making renewal projects possible as funds became available for them. Construction provided jobs for the unemployed. In the early 1940's workers migrated to the cities for war jobs, but the absence of men in the Armed Forces and the shortage of construction materials brought renewal work to a stop. The end of the war saw the return of servicemen but no return to rural living, so cities suddenly needed more housing. Slum clearance then proceeded at such a pace that officials seldom took time to think of the poor people replaced. These moved to neighborhoods they couldn't afford to keep up and gradually turned them into new slums.

From the end of the war to the late 1960's almost every city in the United States and Canada undertook renewal work. The automobile, which helps people to live conveniently in suburbs, contributed greatly. Planners considered population shifts to the suburbs as beneficial for a city. In theory, modestly well-to-do people moved out, leaving good apartments available for upper-middle-income families. When these moved in, they opened places for lower-middle-income groups, who then left space to be occupied by upper-low-income families. With these moving, adequate facilities became available to the poorest citizens. Once they had moved, the city could tear down the slum they had vacated and turn it into apartments or town houses for more of the upper-middle-class people. The cycle would continue until all slums had been eliminated and everybody could live happily ever after. Unfortunately this filtering process, as it was called, failed to work. Residents were not waiting for better living quarters to become available. For the most part, they lived in what they could afford. And landlords, far from reducing rents to lure lower-income groups, generally raised rents to improve their own incomes.

Another planning theory said that neighborhoods would be kept up better if they had an economic mix— that is, if they included families of all income levels. City officials arranged to replace slums with residences of varying rent levels without considering that nearly all the people forced to move from the slum had low incomes. Many would be unable to return, for the economic-integration scheme provided fewer low-income accommodations than had been destroyed. Economic integration often meant racial integration, for low-income families frequently include blacks and sometimes Orientals. Where people objected to racial integration, the expensive facilities stood vacant, deteriorating until their rents came down within the reach of people from lower-income groups. This defeated the economic-mix idea.

By the late 1960's planners argued over the value of urban renewal. Robert C. Weaver, first secretary of the U. S. Department of Housing and Urban Development, thought some of it proved worthwhile and that much more could be made to do so. Nathan Glazar, a critic and author, took an opposing view. Instead of arguing, some planners sought ways to remove slums without completely

144

disrupting the lives of hundreds of families. In a few cities, officials experimented with improving apartment buildings while people were still living in them. Such work may progress slowly, but the increases in rent that result are smaller than when buildings are completely replaced. The families undergo some discomfort, but less, as a rule, than if they move out, wait for a new building, and then move back. Many planners think this type of rehabilitation will take the place of renewals by the 1980's.

St. Louis, Missouri, provided an example of what can happen when planners rely on theories and neglect consideration of people. In the 1950's the city started the Pruitt-Igoe housing project, a complex that eventually included about forty buildings of eleven stories each. They provided accommodations for ten thousand slum dwellers. Looking at the slum to be replaced, planners said the people needed indoor plumbing, clean and colorful buildings, and an absence of commercial enterprises (shops and stores were targets for robberies). They built the apartment houses of orange brick, with indoor plumbing, and without stores and shops. As the first ones reached completion, poor people took up residence and discovered drawbacks.

As critics noted later, orange brick can be colorful in small quantities and overbearing when used extensively. Urban renewal always hits elderly people. These senior citizens have fixed incomes—usually social security benefits—and cannot afford to live elsewhere. Many older people at Pruitt-Igoe found elevators frightening. They feared the doors would close on them and break bones, or that the contraptions would crash into the basement. Because some elevators started stalling, residents had reason to worry about using them. Those unable to walk up and down stairs found themselves marooned on their floors or in the lobby. Those able to use stairs discovered dangers in doing so. The architects had left little space for stairways, and these narrow, dark passages were like obstacle

145

courses, especially after children used them for play and left toys lying about. The stairs gave drug addicts, muggers, and rapists concealment while they waited for victims. The elevators themselves became hangouts for criminals. Even younger people feared to enter or leave the apartment houses alone. Instead of eliminating crime, the planners had developed a high-crime neighborhood. Without stores nearby, families had to walk many blocks to shop. Unless relatives or friends saw that they received groceries and other necessities, some elderly people had to spend money they couldn't afford for deliveries. Ordering by phone, they ended up with low-quality meats or clothing in wrong sizes.

Many families had come originally from rural areas, where they had enjoyed fields and woods, winding lanes and peaceful bayous. Between buildings at Pruitt-Igoe they found concrete courtyards, with occasional patches of bare ground where the running feet of children discouraged every blade of grass that tried to grow. No magnolia hung with Spanish moss offered cool shade. Instead, the masses of brick and concrete captured the sun's heat and made summers nearly unbearable. In winter, cold winds whipped among the buildings. The people found little pleasure in going outdoors. They also found little pleasure inside. Children burned themselves on exposed pipes. The planners had decided on one- and two-bedroom apartments, neglecting to consider how many families had numerous children. The people felt cramped as well as trapped.

Any family able to move away did so. Whites went first, leaving an entirely black neighborhood. Although a slum bordered the new project, people preferred it to the problems of Pruitt-Igoe. Many apartments in the new area stood empty. Broken windows remained unfixed or were boarded over. Before it was a decade old, the project took on the appearance of a slum itself. Tenants started withholding rents because the housing authority refused to

146

make repairs, and the authority said it lacked the funds for repair work. In 1969 the remaining families staged a rent strike, forcing the city to start replanning an area that had just been renewed.

This time St. Louis decided on rehabilitation instead of renewal. It started on March 16, 1972, when a controlled explosion brought one eleven-story skyscraper crashing to the ground. A few other buildings were also destroyed, opening some much-needed space between those remaining, but mostly the planners intended to do over the twenty-year-old structures. They removed the top floors, leaving apartment houses of three, four, and five stories. The different heights added variety, and healthy people could walk up and down. Thought was given to housing elderly and disabled people on the ground floors. Architects sometimes broke through walls to combine two or three small apartments into accommodations for large families. Stairways became more open and better lighted. Insulation covered exposed pipes. Although the rehabilitated area housed fewer than ten thousand people, it held as many as had been living there by the start of the 1970's, when so many apartments stood empty. The planners also set aside space for two parks, one for children and the other for senior citizens, and turned some ground-floor apartments into shops. The rehabilitated area answered more of the city's needs than had been done by the renewed section.

Officials of some cities say that malls have helped to save the downtown, or inner-city, areas, saving nearby residents from having to depart. After prohibiting traffic on certain streets, the cities provide fountains and other decorative, inviting features, along with comfortable benches on which people can rest, and perhaps even sandboxes in which children can play. If these are well lighted and policed, people feel safe in coming to them. These sections can compete with suburban shopping centers, and local families no longer feel trapped in the inner city or driven from it. Individuals, families, and shopkeepers all feel they escape being forced to move. This type of urban renewal may even encourage families of the city to make repairs and do some house painting on their own. Of course, some mall areas have proved more successful than others.

Santa Cruz, California, has apparently benefited considerably through the building of an inner-city mall. One spokesman there has said, "A well-designed mall with adequate parking, attractive facades, and smart merchandising can compete with shopping centers and remain a healthy core of any community." A pleased businessman reported, "We would have soon gone under if the mall hadn't been built. Now our downtown area is so pleasant and attractive that people come all the way from Monterey and San Jose to shop here."

17
A GLANCE BACK,
A GLANCE FORWARD

In Conclusion

To a degree, urban renewal can be considered representative of forced relocation in general. Where everybody's wishes and needs are considered, it can be beneficial. But if one party has selfish motives, another will probably suffer. Concerned citizens should look for the motives involved when any group wants to move another group, whether temporarily or permanently.

Few forced moves have worked out as well as those involving indentured servants. For communities in Europe, relocation removed people who might have been burdens, nuisances, or troublemakers. For the colonies in the New World, it provided badly needed laborers. And for spirited individuals, it often offered an escape from lives of suffering and want. Historians incline toward the conclusion that in the cases of indentured servants in colonies that became the United States and Canada, forced transplanting was beneficial more often than not.

William King's removal of his blacks to Canada has generally been considered worthwhile, and many of the efforts in relocating people in connection with the Tennessee Valley work and the St. Lawrence Seaway appear praiseworthy. Viewed alongside the unfortunate effects of

149

shifting peoples around, these make a rather small showing.

Could tragedies like those of Acadia, Bikini, and others be repeated? Yes, they could. It seems to be human nature to want to play God. And there will always be people or groups who consider their own interests ahead of those of minorities or the underprivileged. It is to be hoped that North America will never have a Hitler or a Stalin, but their small-scale counterparts exist today all over the world. Studies on aggressiveness and the desire for power may help explain more about why forced relocation occurred in the past and still occurs today. As people understand their motives better, perhaps they will be less pushy or greedy in the future.

BIBLIOGRAPHY

Introduction and Chapter 17

Berger, Josef and Dorothy (eds.). *Diary of America.* Simon & Schuster, 1957.

Lorenz, Konrad. *On Aggression.* Harcourt, Brace and World, 1966.

Marden, Charles F., and Meyer, Gladys. *Minorities in American Society.* American Book Company, 1968.

Chapter 1. Indentured Servants

Ballagh, James C. *White Servitude in the Colony of Virginia.* New York: Burt Franklin, 1969.

McKee, Samuel D. *Labor in Colonial New York.* Port Washington, N.Y.: I. J. Friedman, 1965.

Smith, Abbott Emerson. *Colonists in Bondage.* Gloucester, Mass.: Peter Smith, 1965.

Chapters 2 and 5. Blacks

Katz, William Loren (ed.). *Five Slave Narratives.* Arno Press and *The New York Times,* 1968.

Klein, Herbert S. *Slavery in the Americas.* The University of Chicago Press, 1967.

Mannix, Daniel P., and Cowley, Malcolm. *Black Cargoes: A History of the Atlantic Slave Trade.* The Viking Press, 1962.

Spears, John R. *The American Slave Trade.* Williamstown, Mass.: Corner House Publishers, 1970.

Chapters 3 and 6. Indians

Brown, Dee. *Bury My Heart at Wounded Knee.* Holt, Rinehart & Winston, 1970.

Debo, Angie. *The Road to Disappearance.* University of Oklahoma Press, 1941.

Grant, Foreman. *The Last Trek of the Indians.* Russell & Russell, 1972.

Oswalt, Wendell H. *This Land Was Theirs.* John Wiley & Sons, 1973.

Pratt, Richard Henry. *Battlefield and Classroom.* Yale University Press, 1964.

Wissler, Clark. *Indians of the United States.* Doubleday & Company, 1966.

Chapter 4. Acadians

Clark, Andrew Hill. *Acadia.* University of Wisconsin Press, 1968.

Longfellow, Henry Wadsworth. *Evangeline: A Tale of Acadie.* Boston: W. D. Ticknor, 1847.

Rawlyk, George A. *Nova Scotia's Massachusetts.* Montreal: McGill-Queen's University Press, 1973.

Chapter 5. See Chapter 2.

Chapter 6. See Chapter 3.

Chapter 7. Mormons

Carmer, Carl. *The Farm Boy and the Angel.* Doubleday & Company, 1970.

Fife, Austin and Alma. *Saints of Sage and Saddle.* Indiana University Press, 1956.

Flanders, Robert Bruce. *Nauvoo: Kingdom of the Mississippi.* University of Illinois Press, 1965.

Taylor, Samuel W. *Nightfall at Nauvoo.* The Macmillan Company, 1971.

Chapter 8. William King

Gregg, William R. *The African in North America.* Ashtabula, Ohio: Brooks Print Shop, 1933.

Jamieson, Annie S. *William King: Friend and Companion of Slaves*. Toronto: Missions of Evangelism, 1925.

Stowe, Harriet Beecher. *Dred: A Tale of the Great Dismal Swamp*. Houghton Mifflin Company, 1885.

Chapter 9. Jews

Catton, Bruce. *Grant Moves South*. Little, Brown & Company, 1960.

Grant, Ulysses S., 3d. *Ulysses S. Grant, Warrior and Statesman*. William Morrow & Company, 1969.

Chapter 10. Métis

Berton, Pierre. *The Impossible Railway*. Alfred A. Knopf, 1972.

Howard, Joseph K. *Strange Empire*. William Morrow & Company, 1952.

Osler, Edmund Boyd. *The Man Who Had to Hang*. Toronto: Longmans, Green & Company, 1961.

Chapter 11. Company Towns

Allen, James Brown. *The Company Town in the American West*. University of Oklahoma Press, 1966.

Warne, Colston E., and others. *The Pullman Boycott of 1894*. D. C. Heath & Co., 1955.

Wolff, Leon. *Lockout*. Harper & Row, 1965.

Chapter 12. TVA

Billings, Henry. *All Down the Valley*. The Viking Press, 1952.

Davidson, Donald. *The Tennessee*. Holt, Rinehart & Winston, 1946.

Droze, Wilmon H. *High Dams and Slack Waters*. Louisiana State University Press, 1965.

Mabee, Carleton. *The Seaway Story*. The Macmillan Company, 1961.

Chapter 13. Japanese Americans

Conrat, Maisie and Richard. *Executive Order 9066*. California Historical Society, 1972.

Okamoto, Daniel I. *American in Disguise*. Walker/Weatherhill, 1971.

153

Spicer, Edward H., and others. *Impounded People.* University of Arizona Press, 1969.

Chapter 14. Bikini
Cameron, James. "Twenty-three Nuclear Explosions Later," *The New York Times Magazine,* March 1, 1970, p. 24.
Shurcliff, William A. *Bombs at Bikini.* Wm. H. Wise & Company, 1947.

Chapter 15. Vietnam
Fall, Bernard B. *The Two Viet-Nams.* Frederick A. Praeger, 1967.
Hammer, Richard. *One Morning in the War.* Coward-McCann, 1970.
Schell, Jonathan. *The Village of Ben Suc.* Alfred A. Knopf, 1967.

Chapter 16. Urban Renewal
Goodman, Robert. *After the Planners.* Simon & Schuster, 1971.
Lowe, Jeanne R. *Cities in a Race with Time.* Random House, 1967.
Weaver, Robert C. *Dilemmas of Urban America.* Harvard University Press, 1965.

Chapter 17. See Introduction.

INDEX

155

158